KRIEGSMARINE NORWAY COMMAND 1940–45

The naval war on the northern flank

Lawrence Paterson
Illustrated by Edouard A. Groult

OSPREY PUBLISHING
Bloomsbury Publishing Plc
Kemp House, Chawley Park, Cumnor Hill, Oxford OX2 9PH, UK
Bloomsbury Publishing Ireland Limited,
29 Earlsfort Terrace, Dublin 2, D02 AY28, Ireland
Bloomsbury Publishing Inc.
1359 Broadway, 12th Floor, New York, NY 10018, USA
E-mail: info@ospreypublishing.com
www.ospreypublishing.com

First published in Great Britain in 2026

A catalogue record for this book is available from the British Library.

ISBN: PB 9781472871084; eBook: 9781472871091; ePDF: 9781472871060; XML: 9781472871077

26 27 28 29 30 10 9 8 7 6 5 4 3 2 1

Maps by bounford.com
Diagrams by Adam Tooby
Index by Richard Munro
Typeset by Lumina Datamatics Ltd
Printed by Repro India Ltd.

MIX
Paper
FSC FSC® C047271

Osprey Publishing supports the Woodland Trust, the UK's leading woodland conservation charity.

To find out more about our authors and books visit www.ospreypublishing.com. Here you will find extracts, author interviews, details of forthcoming events and the option to sign up for our newsletter.

For product safety-related questions contact productsafety@bloomsbury.com

CONTENTS

THE FLEET'S PURPOSE

BACKGROUND

Kriegsmarine units based in or operating from Norway between 1940 and 1945 did not constitute a single fleet. Rather, we are examining those formations that were controlled by Commanding Admiral, Norway, or which were under the direct authority of *Marinegruppenkommando Nord.* Initially, possession of the Norwegian harbours seemed to offer great offensive possibilities for successful raider voyages into the North Atlantic and beyond.

From the first days of German occupation in April 1940 through to the end of the war, Kriegsmarine regional commands in Norway exercised operational control of all naval forces that were based there. Hitler had originally harboured no intentions of seizing Norway. However, following the Soviet Union's attack on Finland in late 1939, fears in Berlin of a potential British landing in Norway grew exponentially. Under the guise of military aid for Finland, British landings in northern Norway, subsequent occupation and direct pressure then applied to Sweden were accurately viewed as a genuine threat to German interests. Kriegsmarine commander-in-chief Grossadmiral Erich Raeder was particularly concerned, acknowledging that during World War I, the Royal Navy had been able to contain Imperial Germany's fleet with a combined naval cordon from the Shetland Islands to Norway's coast and a thick mine barrage. Raeder was determined to avoid a repeat of this, and the most logical method of doing so was to secure Germany's northern flank with a subjugated Denmark and Norway, liberating the exit to the 'little pond' of the Baltic.

Furthermore, Norway represented an Achilles Heel for the German war effort. The Wehrmacht was heavily dependent on raw materials imported from Scandinavia. Over half of the iron-ore imported was transported from Sweden's Gällivare and Kiruna mines via Narvik. German occupation of neutral Norway – framed as a 'protective measure' to counter identical British plans – would also provide ice-free northern harbours in proximity to critical North Atlantic sea lanes, allowing U-boats and surface craft to intensify their attacks on Britain's convoy traffic. By contrast, Allied occupation would effectively bar the North Atlantic approaches, threaten the entrance to the Baltic Sea, choke Swedish imports and possibly even swing Sweden into the war on the side of the Allied powers.

Though some within the Kriegsmarine Staff believed it improbable that Great Britain was planning or even capable of such an operation, Hitler fully endorsed Raeder's viewpoint and invasion was hastily scheduled for April 1940. The subsequent Operation *Weserübung* was the largest amphibious invasion ever mounted by Germany and tested its navy to the utmost. Denmark was overrun instantly and, beneath the noses of the powerful British fleet, the Kriegsmarine was able to land assault troops at major ports, including Narvik. Though ultimately successful, casualties were extreme and far-reaching effects on the Kriegsmarine were felt for months to come.

The seriously depleted Kriegsmarine established itself within this newly occupied territory, though slender naval forces were now stretched along the newly conquered Western European coastline that ultimately extended from Norway's Arctic region to the Spanish border. Initial 'coastal defence' units were created, tasked primarily with local minesweeping, patrolling and anti-submarine work. The infrastructure of naval deployment in Norway was rapidly moved into position as, although Norway did not feature heavily in planned surface ship deployments until the following year, it provided an important refuelling stop for heavy units attempting to break through the Denmark Strait into the Atlantic.

Access to the North Atlantic was eased considerably with the acquisition of Norwegian harbours, but the demands on security units to provide escort and protection also increased dramatically. Security flotillas were quickly established to help counter the threat of Allied incursions into Norwegian waters, and extensive defensive minefields were laid. The Kriegsmarine now possessed a strategically advantageous launching point from which U-boats and surface raiders could enter the North Atlantic, with the added proximity of repair facilities shortening rotation times to and from the front. Heavy surface ships, soon stationed in Norwegian fjords, posed a persistent significant threat to Allied operations. Although these units were frequently hamstrung by overly cautious operational guidelines, their very

Generaladmiral Hermann Boehm is welcomed by Hans Joachim von Neuhaus from the German Legation in Oslo and (on the right) Oberstleutnant Hartwig Pohlman at Fornebu Airport, 10 April 1940. (Riksarkivet/The National Archives, Norway)

presence tied down substantial Allied naval resources to counter the perceived danger. Royal Navy battleships, aircraft carriers, cruisers and destroyers were all held for convoy protection in Arctic waters.

Though there were indeed successful future raider forays after German forces installed themselves in 1940, hindsight tells us that the high-tide of such operations was already extremely close. The *Panzerschiffe* (armoured ship, or heavy cruiser/pocket battleship) *Admiral Scheer* remained the most successful such surface raider after sinking 15 ships and capturing two others during a voyage within the Atlantic and Indian oceans that began in October 1940 and ended in Bergen on 30 March 1941.

However, despite the strategic advantages to an occupied Norway, Hitler's fixation on potential Allied invasion of this territory remained a profound disadvantage for the Wehrmacht, stoked to fever pitch by British aerial and commando raids that began in 1940. Fearing the fragility of German control over the vital iron ore export route, a stream of almost constant reinforcement of all three Wehrmacht services flowed into Germany's occupation force, taking them away from active battlefields where they were sorely needed.

When Germany attacked the Soviet Union in June 1941, as well as eventual attempts to intercept British PQ convoys carrying military supplies and equipment bound for Russian Arctic ports, northern-based Kriegsmarine units were tasked with supporting the major ground offensive towards Murmansk as well as stopping subsequent Soviet landings behind the German front line dangerously close to Finland's nickel mines at Petsamo.

The Soviet Union's Arctic coastline is extremely harsh. It is icebound during the winter, apart from a 70-mile stretch of the Kola Peninsula that includes the ports of Murmansk and Pechenga, warmed by the Gulf Stream all year round. These were the primary disembarkation ports for supply convoys from Britain. During the summer months between May and August, the sun shone 24 hours a day, while in winter it did not rise above the horizon between mid-November and mid-January.

The fighting on land between German and Soviet troops in the far north soon degenerated into static trench warfare. The Kriegsmarine was fully utilized to keep struggling German units supplied while coming under intense pressure from the energetic Soviet Northern Fleet, which also mounted counter-attacks by landing marines behind beleaguered German mountain troops.

Despite its strategic positioning, the primary role that German naval units found themselves fulfilling was one of supply and convoy defence. Convoys carrying Sweden's iron-ore were routed to Rotterdam, from where the cargoes could be transhipped to barges and carried onwards to the armaments factories within the Ruhr Valley.

Early British attempts to attack this convoy traffic were handled by an unprepared RAF Coastal Command which was largely equipped with slow

Admiral Hipper and two escorting destroyers putting to sea from Norway, photographed from *Tirpitz*. (Naval History and Heritage Command)

Lockheed Hudson bombers and Bristol Beaufort torpedo bombers. During February 1941, Coastal Command was placed in large part under the operational control of the British Admiralty. The Royal Air Force had not entered the war with any defined anti-shipping doctrine, but rather had concentrated upon the task of strategic bombing while the Royal Navy blockaded Germany. Coastal Command had been created in 1936 as a defence against U-boats that had been so successful against British mercantile traffic during the previous war. Once hostilities commenced, it become rapidly apparent that the Royal Navy was stretched to its limits in all theatres, and Coastal Command's remit was extended to attacking Germany's convoy routes.

Throughout 1940, their results had been dismal despite their best efforts, with 161 aircraft lost for the sinking of only six ships and another 14 damaged. Outdated equipment, lacklustre intelligence, poor serviceability of machines, low morale and a lack of cohesive tactical method had combined to defeat Coastal Command efforts almost as much as minesweepers, *Vorpostenboote* (patrol boats) and Sperrbrecher minesweeper escorts. During these early years, escorting Kriegsmarine vessels provided crucial anti-aircraft support, bolstered by ground-based flak positions and Luftwaffe units stationed in Norway. Naval coastal artillery and flak artillery units were installed along the length of the Norwegian coastline, each unit controlled by the geographical sub-commands held by admirals subordinate to Admiral Hermann Boehm's office. The German Army also constructed coastal artillery and supporting units, which culminated in Norway becoming one of the most heavily fortified parts of Hitler's Atlantic Wall, named *Festung Norwegen* (Fortress Norway). At its peak, 400,000 Wehrmacht servicemen of all three branches were stationed in Norway.

FLEET FIGHTING POWER

WARSHIPS

Battleships, Heavy Cruisers and Light Cruisers

The history of those major surface ships stationed in Norwegian waters has been covered in previous volumes, *Kriegsmarine Atlantic Command* and *Kriegsmarine North Sea Command*, which look at the building of these ships and their service between 1939 and 1942.

The largest ship to be built by the Kriegsmarine was *Tirpitz*; sister-ship to *Bismarck* and the second of its class to be built. Laid down in Wilhelmshaven on 2 November 1936, the ship was launched on 1 April 1939 and commissioned into the navy on 25 February 1941. Like *Bismarck*, *Tirpitz*'s main batteries mounted eight 38cm SK C/34 guns in four twin turrets. Secondary guns were 12 15cm SK C/28 guns, heavy flak weapons 16 10.5cm L/65 guns and lighter flak weapons 16 3.7cm L/83 guns, with 12 2cm C/30 anti-aircraft guns initially fitted, though this number would eventually rise to 58. Main and secondary guns were directed by three fire-control director stations, on top of each of which was a rangefinder in a rotating cupola. After 1942, eight 53.3cm torpedo tubes were installed in two quadruple mounts, one mount on each side of the ship. Four Arado Ar 196 floatplanes were carried. Wartime modifications resulted in *Tirpitz* being 2,000 tons heavier than *Bismarck*, displacing 52,600 tons under full load, making it the largest ship built by any European navy.

Almost identical to *Bismarck*, *Tirpitz* measured 251m in length, with a beam of 36m and draft of 10.6m. Powered by three Brown, Boveri & Cie geared steam turbines, which each drove a screw propeller, the ship was capable of a maximum speed of 30.8 knots on speed trials. The standard crew numbered 103 officers and 1,962 enlisted men, though this was later increased to 108 officers and 2,500 men. Kapitän zur See Karl Topp was captain until February 1943. Originally, *Tirpitz* was intended to make an Atlantic raiding foray in company with heavy cruiser *Admiral Scheer*, but Hitler's direct orders forbade this. Instead, they were destined for Norway.

Destroyers

Destroyers were used extensively in Norway, predominantly as convoy escorts or covering screens for major ship sorties. One of their primary tasks within the North Sea during the war's early years had been minelaying, but this was predominantly left to actual minelaying ships within Norwegian waters. Destroyer flotillas could act as a cohesive unit but were also formed into ad-hoc battlegroups, dependent on ship serviceability and availability at the time of any given operation.

Destroyers had taken heavy losses in Narvik during Operation *Weserübung*. The first unit assigned to Norway following its capitulation was the 6th Destroyer Flotilla, comprising Type 34A and 36 model destroyers. The Type 34A (*Z5 'Paul Jacobi' – Z16 'Friedrich Eckholdt'*), a compromise between speed, range and offensive striking power, displaced 1,850 tons and carried a main armament of five 12.7cm SK C/34 guns, two quadruple 53.3cm torpedo tube installations, four 3.7cm SK C/30s in twin mountings and six individually mounted 2cm C/30 flak weapons. Four depth charge launchers on each side of the rear deckhouse were augmented by six individual racks on each stern flank, and either 32 or 64 depth charges could be carried. Stern rails allowed minelaying, with 60 able to be carried. The ships were powered by what turned out to be untried and highly temperamental high-pressure Wagner steam turbines that caused repeated problems during their operational lifespan.

Unfortunately, their seakeeping qualities were below expectations, being top heavy, difficult to handle and 'wet' in heavy seas. Such deficiencies resulted in a fresh design, the Type 36 (*Z17 'Diether von Roeder' – Z22 'Anton Schmitt'*). These had top-weight reduced, an increased beam, greater bow sheer (the final three being given 'clipper bows') and a slightly reworked hull shape. Though they retained the overly complicated and troublesome steam turbine systems, the Type 36 was a marked improvement, with the larger hull providing increased fuel bunkerage and therefore greater operating range.

The next step in the design chain came with the Type 36A (Z23–Z30, reverting to the tradition of not naming ships of this size), which was, once again, a slightly modified version of the previous class. Eight were commissioned by November 1941, and they were slightly larger in anticipation of being fitted with bigger main guns. Five 15cm TBK C/36 guns were intended to be installed, two in a double turret at the bow and three in single turrets, but a shortage of the required double turrets meant that seven of the eight destroyers sailed with four main guns and a single open-shield gun in the bow Number 1 position (Z23 was the exception, the double turret installed during a refit in 1942). However, all Type 36A ships showed even worse handling characteristics than their predecessors due to the extra armament weight. When Z23 sailed with its double turret, the ship's performance reached a critically bad level, and the installation of further double turrets was abandoned. Continuing design alterations resulted in the Type 36A (Mob) model (Z31–Z34, Z37–Z39 and Z43), with an altered internal layout and a large clinker screen added to the forward funnel, three of which saw action in Norway.

Flak Ships

The Kriegsmarine captured two Norwegian *panzerskipet* (armoured ships) that resembled pre-dreadnought battleships but were officially known as coastal defence vessels. Both HNoMS *'Harald Haarfagre'* and sister-ship *Tordenskjold* had been launched in 1897 and commissioned into the Royal Norwegian Navy the following year. Displacing 3,920 tons, they were 92.66m in length with a beam of 14.78m, well suited for navigating the confined waters of Norway's rugged coastline, though with relatively low freeboard and flush deck they were unsuited to the open sea. The coal-powered steam engines provided only 16.9 knots maximum speed.

By the time of *Weserübung*, both ships had been retired, their main armament removed and used ashore as coastal batteries. Upon seizure by the Germans, they were subjected to thorough structural examinations and engine tests before being taken to Kiel for modernization and rearmament as flak ships.

Their displacement rose to 3,858 tons after being equipped with six twin 10.5cm Flak 38 cannon (*Nymphe* carrying only five twin mounts), two Bofors 4cm flak guns and 14 2cm Flak 30 weapons. The ship bridges were modernized, communications equipment installed and 3m rangefinders fitted for fire control. Tall circular platforms before and aft the funnel each supported a single searchlight, the forward one later changed for two smaller lights. *Harald Haarfagre* was recommissioned as *Thetis* and *Tordenskjold* as *Nymphe* on 1 February 1941, each crewed by 250 men. While the concept of moored flak ships was not new to the Kriegsmarine, these were the only such vessels capable of moving under their own steam.

Nymphe was first used to plug a gap in air defences in the middle of the Elbe River between Cuxhaven and Friedrichskoog. Eventually replaced by an artificial island, *Nymphe* left Cuxhaven on 5 May 1942 and moved first to Narvik, subordinated to Marineflakabteilung 710 and transferred to the Altafjord in April 1943 to protect *Tirpitz*.

Following the loss of *Scharnhorst* in December 1943, *Thetis*, subordinated to Marineflakabteilung 709 in Harstad, was moored in Skillefjord, guarding the narrow entrance to Altafjord. Both flakships moved with *Tirpitz* to Tromsø in October 1944, though they were unsuccessful in preventing the battleship's loss to bombing on 12 November 1944. Thereafter, *Thetis* moved to Kilbotn Bay, south of Harstad, where it ended the war.

Gunboats

In November 1938, the Kriegsmarine ordered four 2,550-ton Colonial Gunboats (*Kolonialkanoneboot*) to be designated K1–K4. Intended to serve in foreign stations of a presumed German colonial empire, policing colonial waters and providing trade protection, the first ship – K1 – was not expected to be completed until 20 May 1941. Subsequently, at the outbreak of war, with German shipbuilding potential already threadbare, K1 was cancelled on 19 September 1939.

Nevertheless, this did not mark the absolute end of Kriegsmarine gunboats. In May 1940, three unfinished K-class Dutch sloops under construction were captured. K1 and K3 had been laid down in Rotterdam, while K2 was in a Schiedam shipyard. Undamaged, all three were completed by the Kriegsmarine and launched into German service; K1 was commissioned on 28 September 1941.

Displacing 1,267 tons and measuring 77.9m long, with a beam of 10.30m and draft of 3.4m, the ships were armed with four Dutch 12cm/45 Mk 8 main guns, as well as four 3.7cm and 12 2cm anti-aircraft guns and a mine-carrying capability. The original Dutch fire control system was retained along with the main batteries, while the remainder of anti-aircraft and anti-submarine weaponry was of German origin. Both K1 and K2 were powered by Germania diesel engines – the same model used in Type VIIC U-boats – while K3 received Humboldt-Klockner-Deutz diesels. All three were assigned to Norwegian waters and acted extensively as convoy escorts. A fourth Kanonenboot – K4, a captured Belgian fishery protection ship – was also commissioned into the Kriegsmarine but served in Channel waters, eventually assigned to the 1st Sperrbrecherflottille.

Captured Torpedo Boats

After *Weserübung*, purpose-built Kriegsmarine torpedo boats of the 1st and 2nd Torpedo Boat Flotillas initially served in Norwegian waters between November 1940 and March 1941. However, with limited wartime resources, the Kriegsmarine also made extensive use of captured vessels. Of six Sleipner-class Royal Norwegian Navy torpedo boats, four were seized during *Weserübung*, classified as destroyers, but akin to the smaller torpedo boats of the major navies, displacing only 735 tons.

Flak ship *Nymphe*, former HNoMS *Tordenskjold*, surrounded by anti-torpedo nets. (Naval History and Heritage Command)

Kriegsmarine gunboat K2, the former Dutch sloop captured while under construction in the Gusto shipyard, Schiedam. The ship was damaged in 1944 by aircraft torpedo attack off Bergen and never fully repaired before the war's end. (Collection: Netherlands Institute of Military History)

HNoMS *'Sild'*, Norwegian 1st class torpedo boat, launched in 1900 and scuttled by its crew in April 1940. Raised and recommissioned into the Kriegsmarine in August 1940 as *Balte*, it served in the Molde Hafenschutzflottille before being decommissioned in July 1944. (Author Collection)

Measuring 74.1m in length, with a 7.75m beam, the ships were originally armed with three 10.2cm guns, one 40mm Bofors anti-aircraft gun, two 12.7mm Colt anti- aircraft machine guns, two 53.3cm torpedo tubes in a twin set amidships and four depth charge launchers.

Gyller and *Odin* were captured without a fight, while *Tor* and *Balder* were both unfinished and captured within their respective shipyards, the former having been scuttled in its dock. Repaired and refitted, all four were rearmed with 10.5cm/45 SK C/32 main guns and commissioned into the Kriegsmarine, now named *Löwe*, *Panther*, *Tiger* and *Leopard* respectively.

Originally grouped into a newly created 7th Torpedo Boat Flotilla in June 1940, they were used as escort ships off the southern Norwegian coast. In December 1940, the flotilla was disbanded and all four ships converted to use as torpedo recovery boats attached to the 27th U-training Flotilla within the Baltic Sea.

The obsolete 578-ton Draug-class Norwegian destroyer HNoMS *'Troll'* was abandoned by its crew at Florø due to lack of sufficient coal to escape to Britain on 4 May 1940, and captured intact by the Kriegsmarine. Recommissioned under its original name, *Troll* was briefly used as a warship before being mothballed, having its superstructure removed and being converted to a water distillation and steam heating supply barge at the *Laksevåg Kriegsmarinewerft* (naval shipyard) near Bergen.

Illustrating the disparate vessels included in Vorpostenboot flotillas, two ageing Snögg-class torpedo boats constructed in 1919 and displacing 256 tons were salvaged by the Kriegsmarine and impressed into service. Measuring 53m with a beam of 5.5m, the ships were powered by two oil-fired shafts and capable of 25 knots. They were armed by two 7.6cm guns and two twin banks of 45.7cm Whitehead torpedo tubes, as well as having minelaying capability with mine tracks fitted on their decks. They are referenced also as Trygg class, entering service in 1920–21.

HNMoS *'Trygg'* and *'Snögg'* were both captured during *Weserübung*. *Trygg* beached after an air attack on 25 April at Isfjorden, while *Snögg* was captured on 4 May in Floro. Recovered and repaired, they were recommissioned as Kriegsmarine vessels *V5503 'Zick'* and *V5504 'Zack'* respectively, both attached to the 55th Vorpostenflottille.

Twelve older torpedo boats of various types that had been constructed between 1894 and 1912 were also captured in Norway. Obsolete, cigar-shaped vessels, they were small and unsuitable for modern torpedo boat use, largely retained for *Hafenschutzflottille* (Harbour Defence Flotilla) service instead, occasionally renumbered as Vorpsostenboote and attached to the 55th Vorpostenflottille.

The most modern and largest of these were the two 130-ton Teist-class vessels that were still in active Norwegian service at the time of the German invasion. HNoMS *'Kjell'* was seized by German infantry on 11 April 1940 and returned to service. Displacing 103 tons, it was armed with two 47cm Whitehead torpedo tubes, a single 7.6cm main gun and 3.7cm flak weapon. The ship was named *Tiger* for four days, redesignated on 23 April Küstentorpedoboot KT1 *(NK01)* of the Kristiansand-Süd Hafenschutzflottille. On 1 October, the ship was outfitted for minesweeping and renamed once more to *Dragoner* (*NK02*). *Dragoner* was sunk by Coastal Command Mosquitos on 28 September 1944 near Kristiansand (known as *Kristiansand-Süd* to the Germans), with seven crewmen killed.

HNoMS *'Skarv'* of the same class of torpedo boat was taken by German forces on the first day of hostilities in Egersund. At approximately 0400hrs on 9 April 1940, German minesweepers M1 and M9 reached Egersund, carrying 40 troops and landing near the moored *Skarv*. The 84-ton Norwegian vessel had been ordered to a state of readiness as events unfolded elsewhere, though denied permission to patrol the harbour approaches. The single

Kjell-class torpedo boat *Dragoner* in Kriegsmarine service, being attacked on 28 September 1944 by Mosquitos of 248 Squadron off *Kristiansand-Süd*. The attacking aircraft is a MkXVIII S/248, armed with 'Tse-Tse' 6-pdr cannons. The torpedo boat was sunk with seven crewmen killed. (Author Collection)

Norwegian sentry aboard *Skarv* mistook the approaching M1 for returning Norwegian destroyer *Gyller*, and a boarding party quickly seized control, though Norwegian crew members managed to destroy maps and important documents before being locked in a shed under armed guard. Once Egersund was secured, *Skarv* was formally surrendered to Eickhorn the following day. The minesweeper then began its return to Kiel, recommissioned on 11 April as NS 01 of the Stavanger Hafenschutzflottille. Later redesignated *NS 28 'Gazelle'*, it was sunk after being rammed by a Norwegian steamer near Lervik.

The oldest example of a captured Norwegian torpedo boat belonged to the Varg class, constructed between 1894 and 1898. Displacing 64 tons under full load, HNoMS *'Delfin'* measured 34.5m in length and was crewed by 12 men. Armed with Hotchkiss machine guns and two bow-mounted 45cm Whitehead torpedo tubes, it was captured while partially dismantled in Kristiansand and recommissioned, serving in the Kristiansand-Süd Hafenschutzflottille as *NK04 'Kürassier'*.

Minelayers

The Kriegsmarine generally considered minelaying to be the domain of existing surface vessels, particularly destroyers and torpedo boats at the outbreak of war. Before long, S-boats and U-boats were also laying mines, the latter more successfully than torpedo patrols during the war's early stages. However, the sheer volume of required defensive and offensive minelaying resulted in the conversion of merchant vessels specifically to minelayers. The only purpose-built minelayer in German possession was the 1,596-ton captured Norwegian minelayer HNoMS *'Olav Tryggvason'*, which surrendered after a confused close-quarter battle in Horten in which *Räumboot* (minesweeper) R17 was sunk and cruiser *Emden* damaged.

Repaired and recommissioned into the Kriegsmarine, the ship was originally named *Albatros II*, before being renamed *Brummer* after an artillery training ship that had been sunk in the Baltic during April. Armed with three 10.5cm SK C/32 guns, two 3.7cm anti-aircraft guns, ten 2cm anti-aircraft guns and four 46cm torpedo tubes, the ship could carry 280 mines laid through three stern launching doors. By 1942, *Brummer* was one of three active minelayers within Norwegian waters, being narrowly missed by six torpedoes fired by Soviet submarine K21 off Båtsfjord, Finnmark, on 9 April 1943.

The 3,071-GRT Norddeutscher Lloyd banana boat *Rapide* was converted to a minelayer in late 1940 within a Danish shipyard, entering the Kriegsmarine as *Ulm* and undertaking its first minelaying mission in Norwegian waters during January 1942. Betrayed by ULTRA intercepts on its fourth Norwegian mission, *Ulm* was sunk by British destroyers on 25 August.

The 5,504-GRT converted steamer *Tannenberg* was *Führerschiff* (command ship) for *Minenschiffgruppe Nord* (Mine Warfare Group North) from November

1940, based in Bergen and Stavanger until May 1941, whereupon it relocated to the Baltic Sea. *Tannenberg* was sunk in a Swedish minefield on 9 July 1941 while operating in support of Operation *Barbarossa*.

The converted 2,436-GRT cruise ship *Roland* was briefly based in Kirkenes, before also relocating to the Baltic, where it was sunk by a mine in April 1944. French cross-Channel steamer *Cote d'Argent* was captured in Saint-Nazaire in July 1940 and converted to a minelayer, being recommissioned as the *Ostmark*. During late 1944 and early 1945, it laid extensive minefields off Norway's northern coast. It was sunk by British bombers in the Kattegat on 21 April 1945. Minelayer *Kobra*, a former 2,130-GRT HAPAG passenger ship, was attached to Minenschiffgruppe Nord from January 1942, laying mines in the Barents Sea east of Poluostrow Rybachi, the most northerly part of continental Russia. Passenger ship SS *'Königin Luise'*, 2,399 GRT, was attached to Minenschiffgruppe Nord after being released from planned *Seelöwe* (Sealion) operations against Britain, laying mines in Norwegian waters before transferring to the Baltic for *Barbarossa*. It was sunk by a mine on 25 September 1941. The 1,281-GRT Danish-built ferry MS *Skagerrak I* was taken as prize in Norway by the Germans in April 1940 and converted to the minelayer *Skagerrak*. During 1942 it was based in Kirkenes, and was sunk on 20 January 1944 west of Svåholmen by Beaufighters from 489 Squadron, RNZAF, while carrying ammunition to Trondheim under escort by M489 and M427.

Minelayer *Brummer*. (Naval History and Heritage Command)

Smaller minelayers and sister ships *Togo* (ex-HNoMS *'Otra'*, 355-ton Otra-class Norwegian minesweeper) and *Kamerun* (ex-HNoMS *'Rauma'*, captured at Horten) were both recommissioned into the Kriegsmarine and used as local minelayers and Vorpostenboote. *NT05 'Togo'* was part

Gunboat K3 in Kirkenes, 1943. (Finnmark Fylkesbibliotek)

of Hafenschutzflotille Tromsø, then Oslo, before becoming *V5908 'Togo'* of the 59th Vorpostenflottille in 1941. *NO 01 'Kamerun'* served in Hafenschutzflottille Oslo.

Security Vessels

The backbone of the Kriegsmarine in all theatres were the myriad security units that provided patrol and picket ships, convoy protection, anti-submarine warfare capability, minesweeping and seagoing anti-aircraft facilities. Of these vessels, the most numerous and multi-faceted was the ubiquitous Vorpostenboot.

Vorpostenboote

One of three warship classes effectively used by the Imperial German Navy for defensive duties during World War I (the others being *Unterseebootsjäger* and *Sperrbrecher*), *Vorpostenboote* (patrol boats) were generally converted trawlers. Germany's trawler fleet had undergone considerable technical development during the 1920s, with improved vessels able to reach as far afield as Greenland. On average, 10 tons of coal and 5 tons of water were consumed daily by a trawler's steam engine to achieve a maximum speed of around 11.9 knots. At the outbreak of war in 1914, most ocean-going trawlers had been commandeered by the Imperial German Navy and converted into Vorpostenboote, successfully combining the tasks of coastal and harbour patrol, convoy escort and anti-submarine missions.

The end of World War I and later onset of the Great Depression caused a slump in German shipbuilding activity, with large shipyards under utilized through a lack of overseas construction contracts or domestic repair work. By 1935, only two shipyards remained active, experiencing a financial boom as a result of the Nazis' accession to power in Germany. The first two ships built after Hitler's inauguration were trawlers, both of which were named after prominent Nazis; the *Carl Röver*, named after the Party Gauleiter of Weser-Ems, and *R. Walter Darré*, the head of the Race and Settlement Office of the SS and Minister for Food and Agriculture. Both ships would later become Vorpostenboote, numbered V209 and V210 respectively during September 1939 and transferred to the 2nd Vorpostenflottille.

Pursuing a greater desire for Third Reich self-sufficiency, Germany's deep-sea fishing fleet was expanded in the late 1930s, with trawlers of 400 GRT displacement becoming a standard design. During 1937, the Kriegsmarine tested the new German trawlers for potential suitability as Vorpostenboote, commissioning five of their own in March of that year so that future models allowed military conversion with minimal work. Germany, one of the world's largest consumers of whale oil, also expanded its whaling fleet with ships built to reach Arctic waters, and these too would later be requisitioned by the Kriegsmarine.

The composition of a Vorpostenflottille varied, dependent upon ships at hand and available armaments. The 15th Vorpostenflottille, which would end the war in Kristiansand, is an example of whalers being used, formed in September 1939 from nine whaleboats (*walfangboote*) that ranged between 348 and 381 tons each. Constructed by Deschimag, these steel-hulled vessels were extremely seaworthy and manoeuvrable, managing a maximum speed of approximately 14 knots. The original crew complement of 15 men was doubled with naval personnel, and the bow-mounted harpoon gun was replaced by a single 20mm C/30 cannon until its slow rate of fire led to substitution with the superior 20mm Flak 38 from 1940. Racks for two to four depth charges were also fitted, although sonar gear was rare.

Trawlers, on the other hand, tended to carry heavier weapons. Typically, they began the war with a single 75mm or 88mm World War I-vintage naval cannon, recalibrated to fire newer ammunition, as well as a single 20mm C/30, with additional lighter machine-gun mountings and the same depth charge complement.

A special class of 'Mob FD' patrol ships was designed in 1940, planned as a potential design on which to base standardized *Vorpostenboot/U-Jäger* (submarine hunter) construction, 21 of them being launched by November 1941. The inspiration lay with the specifications of Norderwerft trawler *Uhlenhorst*, including enhanced compartment division, strengthened stem and stern and a double bottom for about half of the length. These were specifically designed to be converted into trawlers after the end of the war. Displacing 542 GRT, they measured 58.7m long and 8.44m wide, with a draft of 4.4m. Triple expansion steam engines gave a speed of 12.8 knots, and an armament of a single 8.8cm gun, 3.7cm anti-aircraft gun, nine 2cm anti-aircraft guns and six depth charge launchers provided the firepower. However, with an economy under wartime pressure, and shipyards choked with work, only 25 were built by the war's end. Twenty were used as U-Jäger, the remaining five as Vorpostenboote.

Vorpostenboote of 61st V-Flotilla in Oslo harbour, May 1941, showing the distinctive lines of converted Norwegian whalers. *V6107 'Polarkreis'* is closest to the camera and *V6108 'Polarmeer'* alongside. (Finnmark Fylkesbibliotek)

Vorpostenboote were originally controlled by Führer der Vorpostenboote (FdV) West and Ost; the post of FdV Nord was never fully established as an independent command. Those ships that did not comfortably fit within the previous categories – the U-Jäger and minelayers – were directly subordinate to the office of *Führer der Sonderverbände* (Leader of Special Units). However, the command layer of FdV was eliminated in 1942 as unnecessary, its tasks undertaken by regional security commands.

As the war reached its later stages and most Kriegsmarine surface forces were forced to relinquish Western European ports and operational areas, Norway gradually became a 'catch-all' region for virtually every type of German naval vessel. A rarity among these was the short-lived Flakjäger vessel.

Flakjäger

Similar in appearance to the traditional Vorpostenboot – a converted trawler armed and equipped for patrol duties – the Flakjäger were the first such ships specifically designed to counter enemy aircraft. On 25 June 1940, 2. Flakjägergruppe was formed of six vessels:

Flakjäger *Fl.J. 21 'Wiking 8'* (German-built whaler, formerly of 15th Vorpostenboot Flotilla)
Flakjäger *Fl.J. 22 'Wiking 10'* (German-built whaler, formerly of 15th Vorpostenboot Flotilla)
Flakjäger *Fl.J. 23 'Wiking 9'* (German-built whaler)
Flakjäger *Fl.J. 24 'Wiking 6'* (German-built whaler, formerly of 15th Vorpostenboot Flotilla)
Flakjäger *Fl.J. 25 'Yorck'* (Customs launch formerly of 17th U-Jäger Flotilla)
Flakjäger *Fl.J. 26 'Nettelbeck'* (Customs launch formerly of 17th U-Jäger Flotilla)

On 1 November it was renamed 2. Flakjägerflottille; a planned 1st Flotilla for the Baltic Sea was never created as there was deemed no need for anti-aircraft ships there during 1940. Two further vessels were eventually added:

Flakjäger *Fl.J. 27 'Schiewenhorst'* (Trawler)
Flakjäger *Fl.J. 28 'Simon von Utrecht'* (Pilot boat)

The flotilla's original task was escorting convoy traffic between The Netherlands and Germany, equipped during the early war with only a single 3.7cm and 2cm flak weapons and a small number of depth charges. Under the control of Führer der Vorpostenboote Nord, the flotilla would frequently escort vessels between Germany and southern Norway.

By 1943, they had received significantly upgraded flak weaponry as Allied aircraft had become the predominant threat to coastal convoys in all theatres. The four original vessels now carried a single bow-mounted 8.8cm SK C/35 gun (as removed from the Type VIIC U-boats), one 3.7cm and two 2cm flak weapons/ as well as three 15mm machine guns.

However, this armament was at that stage largely mirrored in traditional Vorpostenboote and the like, and on 25 April 1943, the Flakjäger flotilla was disbanded. Of the flotilla complement, Fl.J 25 and Fl.J.26 were both transferred to the 3rd Minesweeping Flotilla, Fl.J. 27 was transferred to the Borkum Hafenschutzflottille and Fl.J. 28 transferred to the 1st Sperrbrecherflottille. The first four Flakjäger retained their original designations and served within the 11th Vorpostenflottille, still under the control of Führer der Vorpostenboote Nord.

U-boats, Type VII

Probably the greatest threat posed to Allied convoys from the Kriegsmarine in Norway was the Type VIIC and VIIC/41 U-boat. However, though great hopes were placed into the establishment of two Norwegian-based flotillas, and the use of U-boats in Arctic waters as part of their outward journey from Germany to France, their potential was never fully realized. U-boats were also a poor reconnaissance platform, their conning towers offering limited sighting range. This role was far more suited to the Luftwaffe, but its limited maritime training and aircraft soon became apparent.

The Treaty of Versailles forbade Germany to possess U-boats, but development had continued in secret, hidden behind a complicated network of fake business fronts and design and testing on behalf of 'client' nations outside of Germany. Raeder established a clandestine U-boat department as early as 1927, and following a series of prototypes built for Spain, Turkey and Finland, three different U-boat types in increasing size gradients were chosen for the Reichsmarine: a 250-ton coastal type, and 500- and 750-ton ocean-going models; becoming the Type II, Type VII and Type I respectively.

The first-generation Type VII was a single-hulled, single-ruddered U-boat with four bow torpedo tubes and one external stern tube. It was popular with crewmen, it was agile and relatively fast on the surface, as well as carrying an 88mm fast-firing deck gun. However, a limited radius of action for an ocean-going U-boat hindered performance, and the single rudder provided insufficient submerged stability.

Design changes yielded the Type VIIB, adding 2m to its length as well as additional 'saddle tanks' of self-compensating fuel bunkers each side of the hull, open at the bottom, allowing diesel oil to float on heavier seawater that entered the tank as fuel was consumed. This Type VIIB U-boat was capable of a range of 6,500nmi at a surface speed of 12 knots, and 90nm at 4 knots

Oberleutnant zur See Helmut Herglotz and the 11th U-boat Flotilla's U290 off the Norwegian coast, 1944. Like most Norwegian based U-boats, U290 sank no ships. The presence of a civilian on the right would indicate that this is likely a shakedown trip to test repairs following an air attack on 14 June that wounded eight men. (Author Collection)

submerged; maximum surface speed increased from 16 to 17.2 knots by adding superchargers to the MAN diesel engines.

Furthermore, the single external torpedo tube was removed and placed internally, firing between the new twin rudder arrangement, which immediately improved the boat's underwater stability and handling. Torpedo stowage was also increased from 11 to 14, with two pressure-tight canisters between the outer deck casing and pressure hull and a further reload stored beneath the decking for the stern tube. Although only 24 of this Type VIIB were constructed between 1936 and 1940, they would swiftly become a mainstay of the early U-boat offensive.

Despite the Type VIIB proving highly successful, the improved model – the Type VIIC – displayed even greater promise. Initial stimulus for the upgrade was installation of new active sonar sound-detection equipment (*S-Gerät*) to augment existing passive sonar in use since 1935. To do so required the control room (*Zentrale*) to be lengthened by 60cm. This allowed enlargement of the conning tower, inclusion of two pressure-tight negative buoyancy tanks to improve diving time, enlargement of the interior fuel bunkers by

GERMAN COASTAL CONVOY ROUTES

Coastal supply traffic was essential for maintaining the Wehrmacht in Norway, moving troops, ammunition, fuel, cement, guns and construction gear between Germany, southern Norway and Finnmark. The *Seetransportchef Norwegen* (Wehrmacht Maritime Transport Chief in Norway) bore responsibility for providing the requisite cargo vessels – typically small to medium coasters and troop transporters – while Admiral der norwegischen Westküste and Admiral der norwegischen Nordküste controlled escort ships and coastal defence forces. Luftwaffe fighters and heavy fighters provided air cover whenever possible.

The main route used by German coastal convoy traffic led port-to-port inside the inner leads: Germany–Skagerrak–Oslo–Kristiansand–Stavanger–Bergen–Trondheim–Bodø–Narvik–Tromsø–Hammerfest–Kirkenes. A number of these ports contained major Naval Service Offices (KMD) and some smaller maritime transport offices (*Seetransportstelle*). Some were merely safe ports with flak and coastal artillery protection that provided sheltered anchorages to stage the journey to the northern regions. Within Finnmark between 1943 and 1945, the Ost/West convoy series were numbered; e.g. Ostkonvoi Nr 110 from Syltefjord in March 1944. Extensive defensive minefields were laid seaward of the convoy routes, protecting fjord entrances.

Supplementing the military convoys, the government-owned shipping fleet Transportflotte Speer was given the job of supplying the Organization *Todt* in Norway, Denmark and Finland. At its peak, the fleet numbered 10,000 personnel, many of them Norwegian sailors who had been trained at a Speer-Schule in Sandefjord. By 1944, the fleet exceeded 2,000 small and medium-sized coastal transport ships originating from Germany, Norway, Finland, The Netherlands, Belgium and France, serving 31 ports across occupied Europe. It had originally been created in 1937 to ferry granite and other materials to Berlin for Speer's urban projects. In Norway it was embedded within the Organization *Todt*'s Einsatzgruppe Wiking, running a coast-long network of shipping offices grouped into three regions: Südnorwegen (Oslo), Mittelnorwegen (Trondheim) and Nordnorwegen (Narvik). It operated a paramilitary rank system, roughly aligned with the Kriegsmarine.

As the threat posed by Allied air power increased, German convoys sailed wherever possible at night or in poor weather, with extra flak protection from shipboard guns installed on merchants and additional escort vessels.

At their peak in 1943, merchant ships carried the following from Germany to Norway:

Coal	2,614,735 tons
Wehrmacht supplies	1,154,750 tons
Cement	142,300 tons
Bauxite	34,200 tons
Mineral oil	36,500 tons
Organization Todt supplies	83,150 tons
Miscellaneous	105,280 tons

From Norway to Germany:

Iron ore	2,244,100 tons
Pyrites	452,100 tons
Miscellaneous	99,530 tons

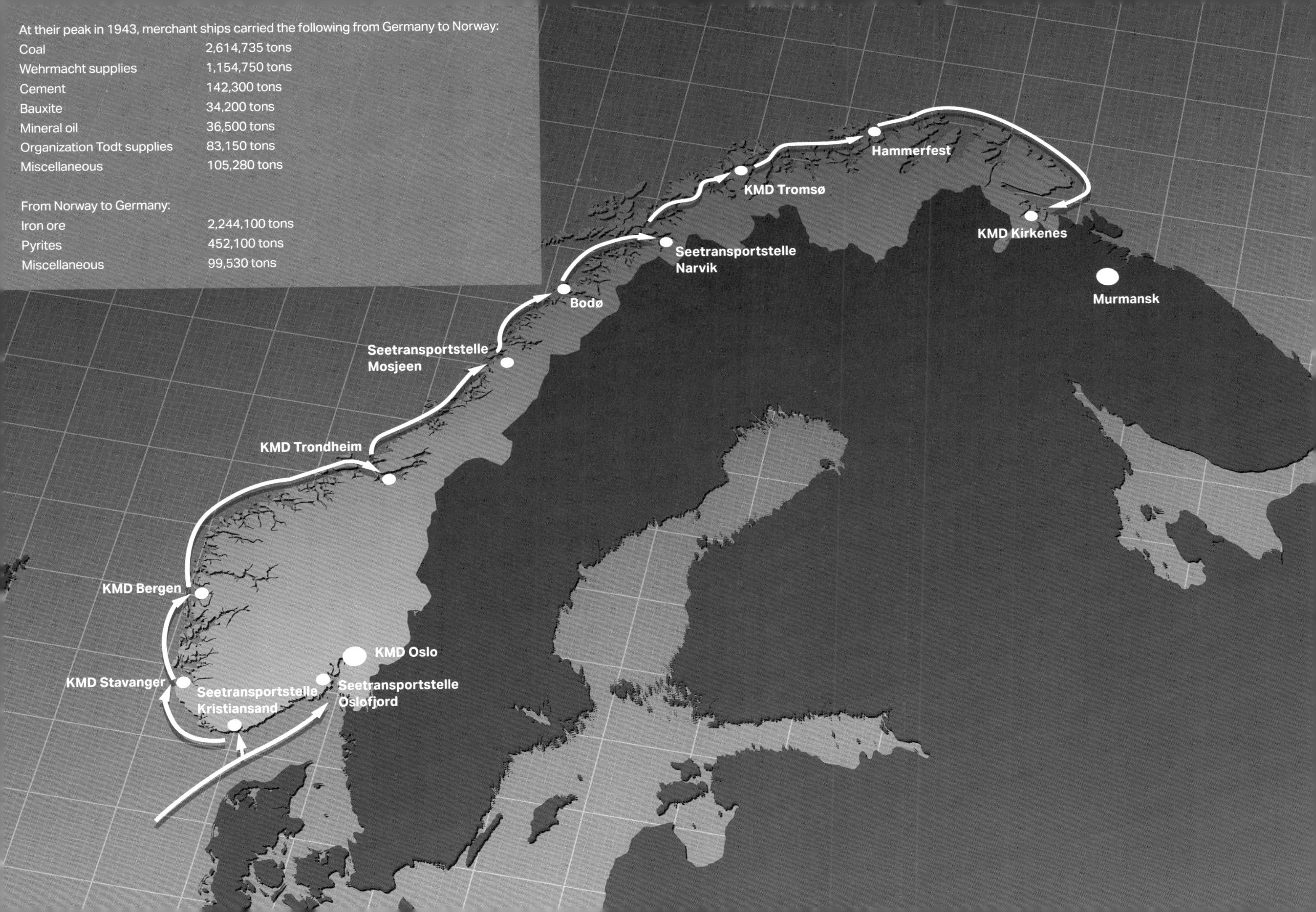

5.4m^3 and engine enhancements. The Type VIIC would soon become the workhorse of the U-boat arm. It too would later receive an upgrade, the Type VIIC/41. This updated design was capable of diving deeper, reducing depth charge effectiveness. With various power and electrical systems replaced by more compact versions, a total of 11.5 tons of hull weight was saved, which converted to an increase in pressure hull thickness from 18.5mm to 21mm, extending test diving limits from 150m to 180m and theoretical hull failure depth from 250m to 300m.

Internally, the pressure hull was divided into three separate compartments by two pressure-proof bulkheads, with watertight bulkheads further subdividing the internal space into six rooms. The stern compartment housed the single stern torpedo and electric motor room and emergency helm. Immediately forward was the diesel engine room, then petty officers' accommodation with eight bunks, the tiny aft WC and a small galley before reaching the *Zentrale*. The latter held navigation and diving controls and conning tower access. The tower was ellipsoid in its aft section and the arc of a circle in the lateral and forward sections, enclosed within an outer casing, its top crowned with the bridge deck of 30mm-thick steel plate, welded to the conning tower walls. Within the pressure hull portion of the conning tower were the aft (attack) periscope with hydraulic driving motor – which was used for submerged attacks – the main rudder steering station and torpedo fire control installation. Externally, the bridge was manned by four lookouts with their own 90° quadrant and a Watch Officer, who maintained the overview. During torpedo attacks, the IWO (First Watch Officer) would man the UZO (*Uberwasserzieloptik*, surface attack optic) while the captain held overall control of events. The stern section of the tower carried the flak weaponry.

Immediately forward of the *Zentrale* was the tiny commander's 'cabin' to port, separated from the rest of the boat by a simple green curtain, lying opposite the information nerve centre of small radio/telegraphy and hydrophone rooms. The officers' and chief petty officers' quarters were next and the forward WC. Finally, the forward torpedo room with its four tubes also doubled as enlisted men's quarters, where most of the crew slept, 'hotbunking' between twelve bunks; one man rolled into the cot to sleep as its previous occupant rose to go on watch. Each man had a small wooden locker in which to store his few personal belongings aboard the boat.

TECHNICAL FACTORS

U-Boat Bunkers

In Laksevåg, a borough within Bergen itself, the construction of the first Norwegian U-boat bunker – codenamed Bruno – had begun in 1941. The bunker comprised six pens – three 'wet' pens, each able to hold two moored boats, and three dry docks for single boats undergoing repair – with associated workshops and fuel and ammunition storage. The advent of the U-boat bunker in Germany, occupied France and Norway was a direct result of the feared impact on U-boat operations from Allied bombing, although Bergen remained relatively untouched until 1944. An ambitious plan to construct Bruno II, capable of holding up to 30 Type XXI U-boats west of Bergen, never materialized.

Bergen eventually hosted a major U-boat shipyard, Kriegsmarinewerft Bergen, with many technical personnel from the Danziger Werft transferred to Norway. To house them and the number of U-boat crews and all ancillary services stationed ashore, camps U-Stützpunkt Lager Prien and U-Stützpunkt Lager Weddigen were built in Laksevåg. Lager Prien alone could house 1,500 men.

Trondheim also had the Todt organization constructing bunkers during the first years of Norway's occupation. Two were planned for the port – Dora I and II – although only the former was operational by the end of the war. The Kriegsmarine took possession of Dora I during 1943, acquiring five pens capable of holding seven boats in total within three dry docks and two 'wet' pens. Dora II was begun in 1942 and was planned to comprise four more pens – two dry and two 'wet' – but was never completed.

Net Barrier Units

The *Netzsperrverband* (Net Barrier Unit) had been established as part of the Kriegsmarine's security forces in September 1939 under the command of World War I veteran Fregattenkapitän Siegfried Tschirch (promoted to Kapitän zur See in October). At its peak wartime strength, the Netzsperrverband controlled over 120 vessels spread between seven regional flotillas and one *Gruppe* in Denmark. Tschirch exercised operational control within the Baltic Sea, while all those units outside of this region were operationally subordinate to the respective local naval commanders.

These flotillas were responsible for the laying and maintenance of anti-submarine and anti-torpedo nets within harbours and approaches. A typical flotilla comprised three to five net-laying vessels and up to 15 net tenders. Armaments aboard such ships varied enormously. While the first net layer, *Genua*, carried only four 2cm flak weapons, *Netzleger II 'Herman Sauber'* carried one 7.5cm gun, two 3.7cm flak guns and four 2cm flak guns.

The first such flotilla to be formed was Netzsperrflottille Nord, created in August 1940, under operational control of Commanding Admiral, Norway, and responsible for net barriers along the entire Norwegian coast. To enable this, the flotilla, under the initial command of Fregattenkapitän Reinhard Emde, was subdivided into five groups:

Group 1 (Kirkenes), responsible for the area of Kirkenes, Petsamo and the Jäniskowski power station.
Group 2 (Narvik), responsible for the area of Kaafjord and Langfjord to Oftenfjord.
Group 3 (Trondheim), covering the area from Oftenfjord to Kristiansund.
Group 4 (Bergen), from Kristiansund to Kristiansand.
Group 5 (Drammen), operating from Kristiansand up to and including the Oslofjord.

While establishing the flotilla headquarters and main storage depot in Trondheim, net layer *Genua*, net tender and converted whaling boat *Netztender 7 'Rau VII'* and buoy tender *Triton II*, along with the coaster *Netze* carrying Luftwaffe supplies, departed Kiel on 8 October 1940 under escort by three auxiliary minesweepers of 11th Minesweeping Flotilla. Spotted off the Lista lighthouse in southern Norway by a British reconnaissance aircraft, destroyers HMS *Cossack*, *Ashanti*, *Maori* and *Sikh* of the 4th Destroyer Flotilla were despatched to intercept, making contact shortly after midnight on 14 October. In a confused melee of gunfire and torpedoes, HMS *Cossack* sank the 1,950-GRT *Genua* with a torpedo, the ship going down with seventy-eight crewmen killed. The 881-GRT Luftwaffe transport *Netze* was severely damaged and on fire; surviving crewmen later evacuated and the ship was sunk by gunfire from minesweeper *M1106 'Roland'*.

To replace *Genua*, the 1,936-GRT *Netzleger II 'Herman Sauber'* was despatched to Norway, followed by *Netzleger XIII 'Deime'* (1,926 GRT). Eventually (and confusingly) a former Soviet heavy barge taken by the Kriegsmarine was commissioned on 25 November 1942 as *Netzleger VI 'Genua'* and assigned to Netzsperrflottille Nord.

The net tenders included within the flotilla were converted whalers *Netztender 7 'Rau VII'* and *Netztender 8 'Rau VIII'*, and converted tugboats *Netztender 10 'Ponto'*, *Netztender 12 'Hast V'*, *Netztender 21 'Fairplay XVIII'*, *Netztender 26 'Otto'*, *Netztender 46 'Rabaul'*, *Netztender 51 'Elsfleth'* and *Netztender 52 'Titan'*. Alongside these were work boats and buoy boats, an example of these being the small, 221-GRT Norwegian steam tug *Bolga*, requisitioned in October 1940 by the Trondheim Harbour Commander (*Hafenkommandant*) and used by Netzsperrgruppe Narvik during 1942, then returned to its Norwegian owners in March1943.

The flotilla's primary task was deploying anti-submarine net barriers across fjords, until 1942 and the arrival of more heavy surface units. These needed 'net cages' (*netzkäfig*) consisting of between two and four rows of net walls suspended from buoys to depths of 18–37m. Concrete base weights laid on the seabed anchored the walls securely.

During March 1943, *Netzleger II 'Herman Sauber'* was assigned to the *Tirpitz* battle group in the Altafjord and Kaasfjord, providing net cages for *Tirpitz*, *Scharnhorst*, heavy cruiser *Lützow*, flak ship *Thetis* and a large naval supply ship. The entrance to Kaasfjord was further secured with a submarine net barrier. Additional net cages for heavy units including *Prinz Eugen* and *Admiral Scheer* were constructed in Bogen Bay, Kaafjord, Langfjord near Alta, Trondheimfjord and Lofjord, as well as a double net barrier at the Barbrudalen Strait. In October 1943, a torpedo net barrier was completed in Langfjordbotn.

The flotilla remained in Norway until the war's end, primarily used for laying anti-submarine barriers at the behest of F.d.U. Norwegen (*Führer der Unterseeboote Norway*) after the loss or departure of the heavy units.

HOW THE FLEET OPERATED

CONTROL AND COMMAND

Kriegsmarine theatre commands were convoluted, 'top-heavy' and frequently revised as the war progressed. At the pinnacle of Kriegsmarine hierarchy was *Oberkommando der Kriegsmarine* (OKM, High Command of the Navy), overtly named in 1935 as Hitler announced open rearmament. Grossadmiral Erich Raeder occupied the Commander-in-Chief position, immediately below him being *Seekriegsleitung* (Naval War Command, abbreviated to SKL), a combined planning and operations department.

Recognizing the complexities presented by geographical dislocation, the first two *Marinegruppenkommando* (MGK, Marine Group Command) offices – MGK West and Ost – were established, immediately subordinate to SKL. Each controlled all Kriegsmarine forces, except for large surface units, within their designated region of responsibility, including security forces such as patrol boats, minesweepers of all types and submarine hunters that were used to safeguard German convoy traffic and the coastal approaches to ports and harbours. MGK Ost was the first to be created in October 1938, with MGK West formed in August 1939.

During August 1940 in a reshuffling of the Kriegsmarine command structure, MGK Ost – responsible for the North Sea – was disbanded and the new MGK Nord established, responsible for the area bordered by a line stretching from southern Greenland to the Northern Hebrides in the north and Den Helder and Cromer in the south. Generaladmiral Rolf Carls established his new MGK Nord command in Sengwarden, and the already established Norwegian naval districts rested beneath his overall command.

Hierarchically immediately below the Marinegruppenkommando came the Naval Region Command – originally known as Marinestation but redesignated *Marineoberkommando* (MOK) in spring 1943. This post became the most senior shore command in any given geographical area, responsible for the administration of all land-based naval assets, including major ports. In total,

Otto Ciliax and Karl Dönitz, photographed in Paris, 1942. Ciliax became Commanding Admiral, Norway in February 1943, remaining in the post until April 1945. (Author Collection)

four naval regions were eventually organized in occupied Europe. MOK Norwegen was not established until February 1943, Admiral Otto Ciliax taking command as Oberbefehlshaber in March and remaining in the post until the final month of the war, when he was replaced by Admiral Theodor Krancke.

Before the advent of MOK Norway, both Norway and Denmark had been officially classed as 'Naval Districts' (the next step down the hierarchical chain from the MOK), with the commanding admiral having direct responsibility for all shore units of the Kriegsmarine and the assigned coastal areas of responsibility, as well as operational command of any permanently assigned surface flotillas. U-boats situated within their sphere of responsibility also answered to the relevant Naval District Admiral, but purely for logistical matters, operational control remaining with U-boat high command (B.d.U.) or regional command (F.d.U.).

Even as Norway was being fought over, the office of *Kommandierender Admiral Norwegen* (Commanding Admiral, Norway) was established as the senior command for the region, redesignated on 1 February 1943 as *Marineoberkommando Norwegen* (Naval Chief Command Norway), and the Commanding Admiral also redesignated as *Oberbefehlshaber* (Commander-in-Chief).

Headquartered in Oslo, Admiral Hermann Boehm occupied these posts until February 1943. He was succeeded as Oberbefehlshaber by Admiral Otto Ciliax (until April 1945) and finally Admiral Theodor Krancke (26 April–May 1945).

Directly subordinate to Marinegruppenkommando Nord, Boehm held responsibility for all of Norway and its coastal area, with four sub-commands established by the year's end for more geographically localized leadership. To handle the complexities of managing a coastline measuring over 25,000kms with its myriad bays, fjords and islands, these sub-commands exercised full operational control over all shore units and any permanently assigned seagoing flotillas, including various types of minesweepers, patrol boats, submarine hunters and harbour defence craft. Each sub-command was controlled by a commanding admiral in charge of sea defences, regional naval shipyards and coastal artillery units, as distinct from operations conducted by MGK Nord, which controlled forces within the North Sea and into the Arctic Ocean.

Subordinate to Commanding Admiral, Norway, were initially three regional commands:

Admiral of the Norwegian South Coast (*Admiral der norwegischen Sudküste*) April–August 1940

Established in April 1940, responsible for the southern Norwegian coast from Kristiansand to the Swedish border. This position was held by Konteradmiral Otto Schenk during its brief tenure. Beneath this hierarchical layer were the offices of a regional naval commander (*Kommandant der seeverteidigung*, Commander of Sea Defences), generally referred to by its commanding officer's title of Seekommandant (comparable to an Army brigade commander), a post generally held by a man of Konteradmiral or Kapitän zur See rank and responsible for harbour defence units, workshop ships and all ground troops within their allocated area, including support and logistics personnel, coastal and flak artillery and marine infantry units.

Schenk's office controlled Seekommandant Oslo and Seekommandant Kristiansand-Süd until his command was dissolved after only five months of activity, Seekommandant Oslo becoming directly subordinate to Boehm as Commanding Admiral, Norway, while Seekommandant Kristiansand-Süd was assigned to the Admiral of the Norwegian West Coast.

Admiral of the Norwegian West Coast (*Admiral der norwegischen Westküste*)

Established on 10 April 1940 in Bergen, with its original geographical boundary from Jøssingfjord in the south to Vinjefjorden near Kristiansund, the post was held by Vizeadmiral (later Admiral) Otto von Schrader for the duration of the war. With the dissolution of the Admiral of the Norwegian South Coast in August 1940, Seekommandant Kristiansand-Süd was also placed under his command and on 1 January 1941, Seekommandant Molde was transferred to the Admiral of the Norwegian North Coast, these territorial boundaries remaining unchanged for the duration of the war.

Von Schrader was initially responsible for Seekommandant Bergen, Seekommandant Stavanger, Seekommandant Kristiansand-Süd and Seekommandant Molde, the latter transferred to Admiral of Norwegian North Coast in December 1940.

Admiral of the Norwegian North Coast (*Admiral der norwegischen Nordküste*)

This office was created on 31 May 1940, formed from an expanded port command and Seekommandant Trondheim, under the command of Konteradmiral August Thiele. Responsibility originally extended from Kristiansund to the Finnish border, but following the creation of the Polar Coast region, its area stretched from Statlandet to Bodø. By July 1940, Seekommandanten Trondheim, Sandessjöen, Narvik and Tromsø had been appointed, with Seekommandant Molde added in December.

In August 1940, as part of the general restructuring of the Kriegsmarine in Norway, the fourth sub-command, **Admiral of the Norwegian Polar Coast** (*Admiral der norwegischen Polarküste*), was established in Tromsø, headed by Vizeadmiral Otto Schenk, who moved from the now defunct South Coast office. Seekommandanten Narvik and Tromsø were transferred to his command effective 1 December 1940, while Seekommandanten Kirkenes, Hammerfest and Harstad were all Schenk's responsibility, bearing the brunt of the war against the Arctic convoys.

Admiral Otto von Schrader pictured on 9 April 1940 during the German occupation of Bergen. Von Schrader held the post of Admiral der norwegischen Westküste for the war's duration. (The National Archives Norway)

The coastal defence districts headed by the Seekommandant were in turn divided into local commands for specific ports or harbours, each directed by a *Hafenkapitän* (harbour captain), the larger of these ports typically hosting a *Hafenschutzflotille* (Harbour Defence Flotilla), generally comprised of commandeered and converted civilian vessels.

Predating the creation of these harbour protection units, from the earliest days of the German occupation, naval commanders began forming *Coastal Protection Units* (Küstensicherungsverbände, KSV), the first of these pulled together by a resourceful officer and former captain of minesweeper M1, Kapitänleutnant Hans Bartels. He created KSV *norwegische Westküste* (Norwegian West Coast) during May 1940, basing his small unit of only four fishing boats and two Vorpostenboote in Bergen, commanding from the headquarters barge *Tan*. Bartels' unit was responsible for local minesweeping, patrolling and ASW (anti-submarine warfare) work, later also adopting the roles of cannon boats and minelayers.

Bartels would soon run afoul of naval bureaucracy while attempting to add improvised but effective elements to his command. He had already managed to accumulate a sizeable force of 45 vessels, which were divided between the 51st, 53rd and 55th Vorpostenflottille and 52nd Minesweeping Flotilla. Bartels recognized the urgent need for small vessels which could operate in shallow water without risk of grounding, and to that end commissioned the construction of 12 diminutive vessels based on Norwegian fishing boat designs and christened *Zwerge* (dwarves). They became the smallest purpose-built minesweepers in German service, weighing only 3.5 tons. *Zwerg 7* was taken to Berlin, where Raeder inspected it, receiving the small crew at OKM headquarters. However, Bartels' independent spirit would be temporarily curbed when he was transferred as Watch Officer to the destroyer Z24 to, as Raeder put it, 'relearn naval discipline'.

During October 1940, Kapitänleutnant Dr Heinrich Behlen was put in charge of *KSV Polarküste* (Polar Coast), based originally in Tromsø with headquarters ship *Nordwind*, before relocating to Kirkenes. Like Bartels' unit, Behlen's flotillas were made up of requisitioned Norwegian trawlers and whaling boats during 1941, responsible primarily for convoy protection. During February 1941, a third region, *KSV norwegischen Nordküste* (Norwegian North

KRIEGSMARINE COMMAND, INSTALLATIONS AND BASES IN NORWAY, JUNE 1942

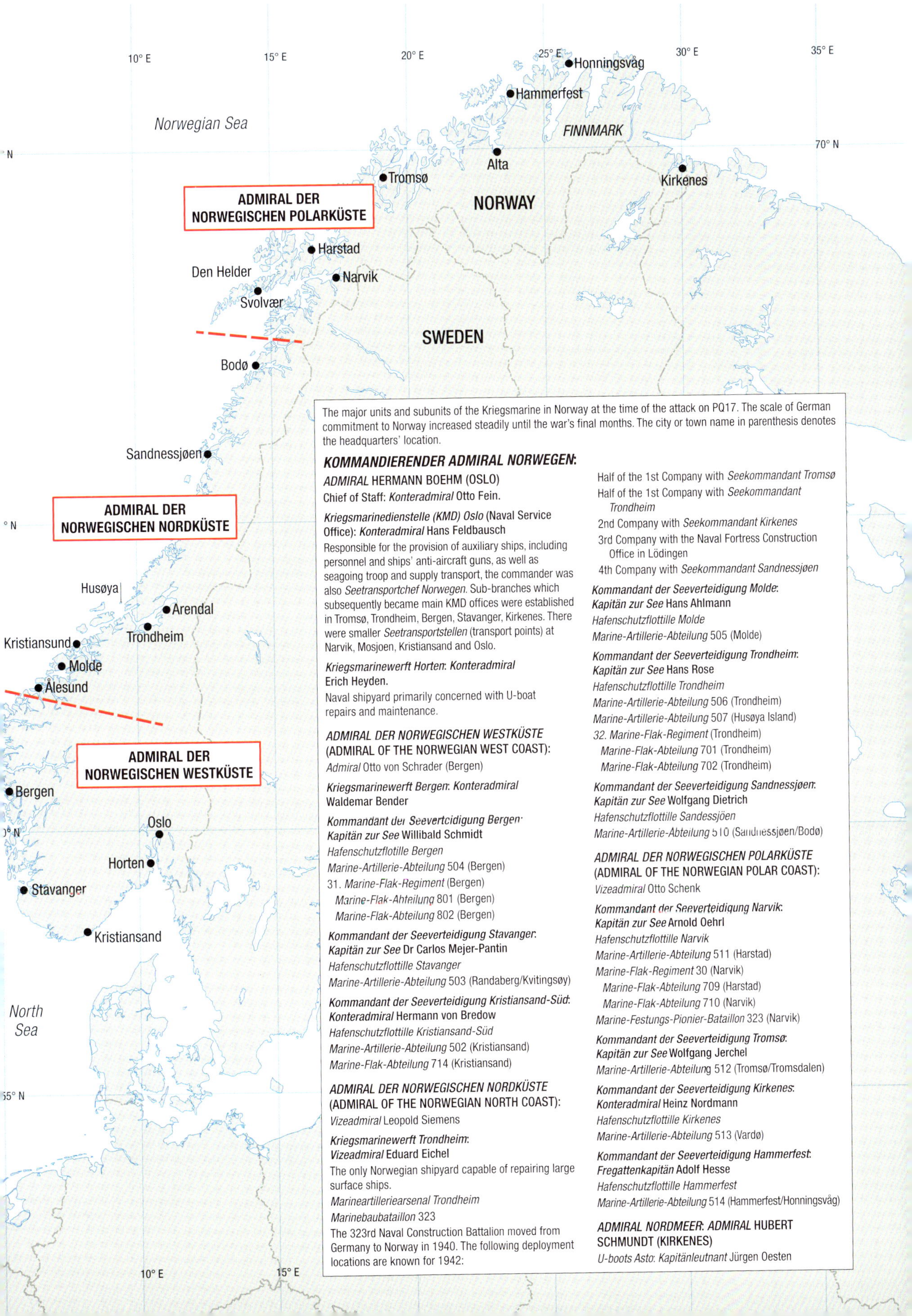

The major units and subunits of the Kriegsmarine in Norway at the time of the attack on PQ17. The scale of German commitment to Norway increased steadily until the war's final months. The city or town name in parenthesis denotes the headquarters' location.

KOMMANDIERENDER ADMIRAL NORWEGEN:

ADMIRAL HERMANN BOEHM (OSLO)
Chief of Staff: *Konteradmiral* Otto Fein.

Kriegsmarinedienstelle (KMD) Oslo (Naval Service Office): ***Konteradmiral*** **Hans Feldbausch**
Responsible for the provision of auxiliary ships, including personnel and ships' anti-aircraft guns, as well as seagoing troop and supply transport, the commander was also *Seetransportchef Norwegen*. Sub-branches which subsequently became main KMD offices were established in Tromsø, Trondheim, Bergen, Stavanger, Kirkenes. There were smaller *Seetransportstellen* (transport points) at Narvik, Mosjoen, Kristiansand and Oslo.

Kriegsmarinewerft Horten**: **Konteradmiral
Erich Heyden.
Naval shipyard primarily concerned with U-boat repairs and maintenance.

ADMIRAL DER NORWEGISCHEN WESTKÜSTE
(ADMIRAL OF THE NORWEGIAN WEST COAST):
Admiral Otto von Schrader (Bergen)

Kriegsmarinewerft Bergen**: **Konteradmiral
Waldemar Bender

***Kommandant der Seeverteidigung Bergen**:*
Kapitän zur See **Willibald Schmidt**
Hafenschutzflotille Bergen
Marine-Artillerie-Abteilung 504 (Bergen)
31. *Marine-Flak-Regiment* (Bergen)
Marine-Flak-Abteilung 801 (Bergen)
Marine-Flak-Abteilung 802 (Bergen)

***Kommandant der Seeverteidigung Stavanger**:*
Kapitän zur See **Dr Carlos Mejer-Pantin**
Hafenschutzflottille Stavanger
Marine-Artillerie-Abteilung 503 (Randaberg/Kvitingsøy)

***Kommandant der Seeverteidigung Kristiansand-Süd**:*
Konteradmiral **Hermann von Bredow**
Hafenschutzflottille Kristiansand-Süd
Marine-Artillerie-Abteilung 502 (Kristiansand)
Marine-Flak-Abteilung 714 (Kristiansand)

ADMIRAL DER NORWEGISCHEN NORDKÜSTE
(ADMIRAL OF THE NORWEGIAN NORTH COAST):
Vizeadmiral Leopold Siemens

***Kriegsmarinewerft Trondheim**:*
Vizeadmiral **Eduard Eichel**
The only Norwegian shipyard capable of repairing large surface ships.
Marineartilleriearsenal Trondheim
Marinebaubataillon 323
The 323rd Naval Construction Battalion moved from Germany to Norway in 1940. The following deployment locations are known for 1942:

Half of the 1st Company with *Seekommandant Tromsø*
Half of the 1st Company with *Seekommandant Trondheim*
2nd Company with *Seekommandant Kirkenes*
3rd Company with the Naval Fortress Construction Office in Lödingen
4th Company with *Seekommandant Sandnessjøen*

***Kommandant der Seeverteidigung Molde**:*
Kapitän zur See **Hans Ahlmann**
Hafenschutzflottille Molde
Marine-Artillerie-Abteilung 505 (Molde)

***Kommandant der Seeverteidigung Trondheim**:*
Kapitän zur See **Hans Rose**
Hafenschutzflottille Trondheim
Marine-Artillerie-Abteilung 506 (Trondheim)
Marine-Artillerie-Abteilung 507 (Husøya Island)
32. Marine-Flak-Regiment (Trondheim)
Marine-Flak-Abteilung 701 (Trondheim)
Marine-Flak-Abteilung 702 (Trondheim)

***Kommandant der Seeverteidigung Sandnessjøen**:*
Kapitän zur See **Wolfgang Dietrich**
Hafenschutzflottille Sandessjöen
Marine-Artillerie-Abteilung 510 (Sandnessjøen/Bodø)

ADMIRAL DER NORWEGISCHEN POLARKÜSTE
(ADMIRAL OF THE NORWEGIAN POLAR COAST):
Vizeadmiral Otto Schenk

***Kommandant der Seeverteidigung Narvik**:*
Kapitän zur See **Arnold Oehrl**
Hafenschutzflottille Narvik
Marine-Artillerie-Abteilung 511 (Harstad)
Marine-Flak-Regiment 30 (Narvik)
Marine-Flak-Abteilung 709 (Harstad)
Marine-Flak-Abteilung 710 (Narvik)
Marine-Festungs-Pionier-Bataillon 323 (Narvik)

***Kommandant der Seeverteidigung Tromsø**:*
Kapitän zur See **Wolfgang Jerchel**
Marine-Artillerie-Abteilung 512 (Tromsø/Tromsdalen)

***Kommandant der Seeverteidigung Kirkenes**:*
Konteradmiral **Heinz Nordmann**
Hafenschutzflottille Kirkenes
Marine-Artillerie-Abteilung 513 (Vardø)

***Kommandant der Seeverteidigung Hammerfest**:*
Fregattenkapitän **Adolf Hesse**
Hafenschutzflottille Hammerfest
Marine-Artillerie-Abteilung 514 (Hammerfest/Honningsvåg)

ADMIRAL NORDMEER: *ADMIRAL* HUBERT SCHMUNDT (KIRKENES)
U-boots Asto: *Kapitänleutnant* Jürgen Oesten

Coast), was established in Trondheim under the command of Fregattenkapitän Alexander Magnus.

The Küstensicherungsverbände were distinct from the Hafenschutzflottillen established in all major occupied ports. The latter utilized whatever local craft they could obtain – from pinnaces, barges and tugs to passenger paddle steamers armed with flak weapons or, at best, a 75mm cannon – to conduct regional surveillance and security.

These would all morph once more in May/June 1944 into six distinct *Küstensicherungsverbände* (Coastal Security Units), two for each of the regional admiral commands. At that point, all existing Hafenschutzflottillen which had operated outside of their remit and directly under command of the relative Seekommandant were converted into Vorpostenflotillen and assigned to the six new units, continuing their responsibility for patrolling, minesweeping and submarine hunting.

Befehlshaber der Sicherung der Nordsee and Minelayers

While 'Commanding Admirals' in Norway controlled security forces within their area, this was not the case for Denmark, where the *Befehlshaber der Sicherung der Nordsee* (B.S.N., Commander of North Sea Security) held responsibility for the North Sea security forces of Danish waters. Beneath the B.S.N. umbrella were also minelaying units.

On 25 November 1940, following abandonment of Operation *Seelöwe* and the release of the minelayers that had been held to sow extensive fields in support of the planned invasion routes towards Britain, Minenschiffgruppe Nord was established under the command of Kapitän zur See Hans von Schönemark. Attached to MGK Nord and operationally subordinate to the B.S.N. (Vizeadmiral Eberhard Wolfram), it was responsible for minelaying in Norwegian waters, generally controlling three minelayers, though this number varied dependent on requirements. The minelayers themselves were frequently rotated between regions.

Schönemark's department was reorganized in April 1942 as it merged with Minenschiffgruppe West, the office redesignated Führer der Minenschiffe, initially directly subordinated to Fleet Command until November 1944, when it was transferred to the control of *Befehlshaber der Sicherungsstreitkräfte* (Commander of the Security Forces), a new office established directly below Fleet Command as regional security commands became defunct and were dissolved throughout a shrinking Reich.

Führer der Minenschiffe:
Kapitän zur See Arnold Bentlage, April 1942–May 1942
Fregattenkapitän Hans von Schönermark, May 1942–February 1944
Kapitän zur See Hugo Pahl, February 1944–May 1945

Admiral Nordmeer and Norwegian U-boat Command

The introduction of U-boats to the war in Norwegian Arctic waters brought the need for a new dedicated command. As part of the Kriegsmarine commitment in support of Operation *Barbarossa* – and much against Dönitz's advice – several Type VIIC U-boats were despatched from Germany to the polar seas to intercept enemy military and merchant shipping in support of a land advance towards Murmansk. Administratively attached to French and German-based U-boat flotillas, the boats were frequently diverted to Norway while en-route to fresh deployments from French U-boat bases. Once within the Arctic, they operated not under direction from B.d.U. but rather directly beneath Boehm's command umbrella as Kommandierender Admiral Norwegen.

In October 1941, an extra command layer was added with the creation of Admiral Nordmeer (literally 'Admiral North Sea', though 'Admiral Arctic Ocean' is more accurate), headed by the former commander of cruisers (B.d.K.) Admiral Hubert Schmundt and established to direct operations of both surface ships and U-boats in northern Norway against Allied convoy traffic. These duties had previously been handled by Einsatz Stab z.b. V., a special staff unit established under Kommandierender Admiral Norwegen to direct U-boat operations in Arctic waters between August and December 1941.

By 20 December 1941, 47 Allied ships had successfully reached Archangelsk in six convoys, only a single ship being forced to return to Iceland after suffering

German convoy viewed from the stern of R202 of the 7th R-Flotilla. On the right, with painted shark teeth, is a minesweeping float from an Oropesa sweep. (Finnmark Fylkesbibliotek)

damage from ice as part of PQ3. Schmundt's new office was established directly subordinate to Marinegruppenkommando Nord, while under instructions from Kommandierender Admiral Norwegen and in cooperation with Army and Luftwaffe units. As well as coordinating U-boat deployment within the Arctic, this included attacking enemy supply lines, protecting coastal transport convoys and defensive minelaying.

However, this breadth of duties proved impractical, and control and protection of German coastal convoys remained the domain of Admiral Polar Coast. The Kriegsmarine began reorganizing its Norwegian command structure and facilities, though, like much of the Third Reich's political and military infrastructure, it remained ponderous and somewhat labyrinthine. The unwieldy chain of command had been complicated by the addition of major surface units after Hitler had ordered the return of capital ships from France to Norway and the transfer of the *Tirpitz* from Germany. These would remain under the command of the Fleet Commander and the Commanding Admiral, Battleships (B.d.S., Befehlshaber der Schlachtschiffe, Vizeadmiral Otto Ciliax), who would be stationed in Trondheim or Narvik. Admiral Nordmeer remained in Kirkenes, and Marinegruppenkommando Nord (Generaladmiral Rolf Carls) would direct forces of the Fleet Commander, while Boehm directed those belonging to Schmundt.

Befehlshaber der Schlachtschiffe had been established in June 1941 as tactical command for Germany's remaining capital ships; the post was redesignated *Befehlshaber der Kreuzer* (B.d.K., Commander of Cruisers) in June 1942 and Befehlshaber der Kampfgruppe in February 1943. Finally, the office was renamed 1. Kampfgruppe in the summer of 1944 before being dissolved on 20 October.

NARVIK

Like most major Kriegsmarine bases in Norway, Narvik's sea and air defences were a mixture of naval coastal batteries (*Marine Küstenbatterie*, or MKB), Army coastal batteries (*Heeres Küstenbatterie*, or HKB) of Heeres Küsten Artillerie Regiment 973 and Luftwaffe flak installations. These evolved as greater resources were allocated and as the most pressing threat changed from seaborne to airborne, though fears of an amphibious invasion remained almost constant throughout the war.

Naval coastal artillery at Narvik was handled by units of Marine Artillerie Abteilung (MAA) 516, formed in Narvik in August 1942 from a cadre centred on 6./MAA 511. It was subordinate to Kommandant der Seeverteidigung Narvik.

Naval anti-aircraft installations were generally attached to the coastal batteries, an exception to this being within Bogen Bay, which had its own anti-aircraft batteries to protect the valuable anchorage and repair ships stationed within it. Marine-Flak-Regiment 30 initially handled the Narvik area with subordinate Marine-Flak-Abteilungen 706, 709 and 710 under Seekommandant Narvik at different times. The regiment was disbanded and its component parts included in Marine Artillerie Regiment 30 established in Harstad in April 1944 under the command of Kapitän zur See Johannes Babel and still subordinate to Seekommandant Narvik. Flak unit rotations meant successive units in charge of the same location over time.

Near the entrance to Ofotfjord

Artillery

MKB 3./516 Lødingen – 4 x 30.5cm H/L 30 Bofors (ex-Norwegian) guns, plus 8.8cm Flak and a 15cm searchlight. Flak 36 guns and searchlight.

MKB 2./516 Tjeldøy – 4 × 15cm SK L/40 C/97 guns, operational by late 1944.

HKB 31./973 Evenestangen – 3 × 21cm Mörser 18 (heavy howitzer).

HKB 32./973 Tjelneset – 3 × 21cm Mörser 18.

HKB 37./973 Ramnes – 4 × 10.5cm K331(captured French).

Torpedo batteries (two at the water's edge: Otofjord entrance)

Torpedobatterie 6./516 Korshavn

Torpedobatterie 6./516 Porsøy

Initially both batteries carried 2 × 50cm G7v torpedo tubes from World War I which were refitted: September 1944 with 2 × 53cm torpedo tubes for standard G7 torpedoes. Each site also had 2 × 2cm Oerlikon flak weapons, light machine guns and searchlights.

Within Inner Ofotfjord and Narvik

Artillery

HKB 33./973 Øyjordneset – 4 × 10.5cm K331 guns (captured French).

HKB 34./973 Rombakken – 6 × 15.5cm sFH 414 (captured French).

HKB 35./973 Saltvikneset – 4 × 10.5cm K331 (captured French).

HKB 36./973 (ex-MKB 3./511) Framnes (Narvik) – 4 × 12cm L/44 Armstrong (ex-Norwegian naval guns).

Kriegsmarine Flak Installations unconnected to coastal artillery

Bogen Bay, west of Narvik – four heavy 8.8cm Flak 36 batteries with searchlights emplaced at Lakså, Tangvik, Østervik and Bergviknes.

Luftwaffe Flak Units

Framnes/Durmålshaugen – 7.5cm flak positions.

Storholtet (Framnes ridge) – 10.5cm heavy flak battery.

Kvitbergan (above Framneslia) – searchlight and 2cm flak weapons, and MG AA positions.

Øyjord/Toppåsen (opposite Narvik).

Not until March 1942 did Dönitz's urging for the creation of a dedicated U-boat command for Arctic operations reach fruition. Veteran skipper and former commander of Brest's 9th U-boat Flotilla, Kapitänleutnant Jürgen Oesten, began serving as *Unterseeboots-Asto* (U-boat Staff Officer) on the staff of Admiral Nordmeer aboard the depot ship *Tanga* in Kirkenes. He would remain at the post until January 1943, when the post of F.d.U. Norwegen was established. Further up the command chain, the veteran skipper and erstwhile commander of La Rochelle's 3rd U-boat Flotilla, Kapitänleutnant Herbert Schultze, joined MGK Nord as Unterseeboots-Asto, also in March 1942.

However, concerns remained over the difficulties caused by U-boat operational control being split between Schmundt's post and Hermann Boehm's Norwegian command. Schmundt's authority – and therefore that of Jürgen Oesten – only covered boats within a central band of the Arctic Ocean, those operating further west falling within Boehm's agency. Both officers agreed that this was unwieldy and untenable. They reasoned that Schmundt's authority should extend over a larger operational area representing an 'organic whole', so that he himself would be in the position to commit forces over a greater region, allowing more streamlined and unified planning. Schmundt's command area was soon extended eastward approximately from the line Lofoten Islands–Jan Mayen and Schmundt was given operational responsibility, guided only by directives from above. The post of Admiral Nordmeer was placed directly subordinate to MGK Nord, thereby eliminating tedious links in the command chain.

Correspondingly, Schmundt and Oesten shifted their command station to Narvik, whose port was considered ideal for the transportation of supplies as it sat at a railroad terminal point. This would become a focal U-boat station for those boats active against Russian forces and the PQ convoys, with the heavily bombed Kirkenes retained as jump-off port and auxiliary base for both U-boats and destroyers. Realism had finally taken hold in OKM, with acknowledgement that U-boats stationed in Norway would be next to useless against any potential invasion traffic and better served in operations against the Murmansk convoys. Concurrently, Kriegsmarine command recognized the likelihood of only sparse results by U-boats in the Arctic during the summer months, with hours of perpetual light. With surface ships limited by scarce fuel stocks, the Luftwaffe was the primary striking force, but U-boats would still be used as much as permissible.

U-boats used within Norwegian waters until May 1942 were generally diverted from transit to the French bases. However, on 15 May the 11th U-boat Flotilla, under the command of Fregattenkapitän Hans Cohausz, was established in Bergen. In June 1943, the 13th U-boat Flotilla was created in Trondheim, formed by the administrative transfer of 12 U-boats which remained operationally unaffected and under F.d.U. Norway direction. Thereafter, Trondheim was increasingly the focal point for Arctic boats while the Bergen's 11th U-boat Flotilla functioned increasingly as transit point for

U-boats headed west. Not until 15 December 1944 was a third flotilla – the 14th – of eight boats established in Narvik. These flotillas did not exercise any operational control over U-boats but rather provided logistical support for boats and crews in harbour and the flotillas' home waters.

The Atlantic U-boat war was already faltering by the beginning of 1943, and in Norway, U-boat operational structure was reorganized once more. Kapitän zur See Rudolf Peters, former *Geneisenau* officer and commander of the 2nd ULD (*U-Lehrdivision*, or U-boat Training Division) and 24th U-training Flotilla, took charge of the newly created post of F.d.U. Norwegen on 18 January, responsible for logistics and operations for the two Norwegian-based U-boat flotillas, the 11th and 13th. His headquarters was aboard the former state yacht *Grille* in Narvik harbour, Jürgen Oesten remaining as Operations Officer until returning to sea as commander of long-range boat U861 in the middle of 1943. Oesten later remembered:

Konteradmiral Otto Klüber, Admiral Nordmeer from September 1942 to March 1944. (Author Collection)

> *'I had several commanders in succession: Admiral Schmundt – an aesthete who was harassed by the commander of MGK Nord, Generaladmiral Carls, in Wilhelmshaven – Konteradmiral August Thiele [from August 1942 to September 1942] and Konteradmiral Otto Klüber (who crawled so far up his superiors' arses that you could only recognise him by the "Dunlop" on the heel of his boot, so we called him "Mr Dunlop"). After the establishment of F.d.U. Norwegen came Kapitän zur See Peters from the torpedo school, an ordinary man with little real U-boat experience.'*[1]

With U-boat responsibility finally separated from Admiral Nordmeer, the latter possessed sparse strength by which to attack enemy convoy traffic. From March 1943, MGK Nord assumed operational control in the Norwegian area and from March 1944, Admiral Nordmeer staff was reduced in size and merged with F.d.U. Norway before being dissolved on 4 June 1944. By that stage, Fregattenkapitän Reinhard 'Teddy' Suhren was F.d.U. Norwegen, appointed in May and holding the post until the war's end.

Landing Craft Flotillas

While attacks on Arctic convoys occupied the offensive capabilities of the Kriegsmarine in Norway, facilitation and protection of German maritime transportation routes was the core responsibility of the majority of Germany's naval presence in the region. The addition of purpose-made landing craft

1 Oesten letter, 24 June 1995, quoted in *Deutsche U-Boote vor Norwegen*, p.36.

(*Marinefahrprähme*, or MFP) to the Norwegian forces not only added relatively cheap escort craft but massively increased short-range troop and equipment transport capabilities.

Marinefahrprähme had been developed for the expected invasion of Britain, displacing 155 tons, constructed of riveted steel with a raised stern and bow complete with ramp. The aft portion of the cargo area was enclosed by a steel roof and three six-cylinder Deutz diesel truck engines were placed in a stern engine room, above which the wheelhouse was mounted; both were protected by 20–25mm armour plating. The craft could reach 10.5 knots but were found to only manage sea state 2 under full load. Marinefährprahme were equipped with MES mine defence, which interfered with magnetic compass navigation, requiring pilot boats to guide them in operation. At first, they were supplied with two 20mm flak weapons but, like most Kriegsmarine security vessels, would be considerably up-gunned as the war progressed. The original crew complement was two officers and ten men.

Several *Artilleriefahrprähme* (artillery ferries) were commissioned into Hafenschutzflottillen during early 1943 to bolster security forces. These were gunboats created by the installation of guns on an MFP, generally numbering two 20mm Vierling flak cannons, one 75mm cannon and two 88mm cannons. The cargo hold was converted into a covered magazine protected by 100mm-thick armour, bolstered by 10cm of concrete filling adjacent bulwarks. The overall increase in weight lessened the Artilleriefährprähme to 8 knots maximum. Of shallow draught, they became extremely effective within inshore waters, their pennant numbers prefixed 'AF'.

8th L-Flotilla

The extreme shortage of patrol craft for Kriegsmarine security units led to the establishment of the 8th Landing Flotilla (L-Flotilla) in Bergen during January 1942. Initially, this unit was equipped only with 'Pmot', a self-propelled barge used as a landing craft and in peacetime for riverine cargo transport. In June, the flotilla received approximately 30 Marinefahrprähme.

After re-equipping, elements relocated to Porsangerfjord in preparation to repel enemy landings in northern Norway. In November 1942, the flotilla was disbanded, the MFPs transferred to the 22nd Landing Flotilla.

MRS 26, 4,010-GRT Norwegian steamer, under construction in an Oslofjord shipyard as a cargo carrier. MRS 26 was one of four captured Norwegian ships converted to use as Minenräumschiffe, combined purpose minesweepers and mother ships for smaller minesweeping pinnaces, carrying a large number of anti-aircraft guns to provide cover for the smaller vessels in operation. Due to production delays, MRS 26 was not in service until 16 June 1944, and was active on the polar coast. The ship was used as a troop transport during the German evacuation of Finnmark when it was bombed. (Author Collection)

The flotilla was re-established in Tromsø in September 1944 and deployed to evacuate northern Finland under the command of the staff unit Landung Einsatzstab Polarküste (Fregattenkapitän Gustav Strempel) created for this purpose. Part of the flotilla also provided additional anti-aircraft protection for the *Tirpitz* in Sandefjord, suffering casualties on 29 October and 12 November 1944. During November, the flotilla ferried 50,000 soldiers and 6,030 vehicles across the Lyngenfjord in 2,130 trips. During 1945, it was used in evacuations from Hammerfest and the island of Söröy.

5th L-Flotilla

The original unit destroyed in the Black Sea, this flotilla was reconstituted in Kirkenes during July 1944 from the remains of 23rd L-Flotilla, under the command of Admiral Polar Coast. Included within the flotilla were a number of Artilleriefahrprähme, some of which had been previously attached to Hafenschutzflottille Kirkenes. It was heavily involved in the evacuation of northern Finland and Lapland, and used to disembark elements of the XIX Gebirgs Korps to counter Soviet landings in Maativnono Bay during October. The flotilla relocated to Honningsvåg to continue evacuation work and then Tromsø, where, during February, it was disbanded and surviving craft were distributed among the 6th, 8th and 9th L-Flotillas.

6th L-Flotilla

Established in June 1944 from the remains of 22nd L-Flotilla, 6th L-Flotilla was based in Hammerfest and mounted transport missions between Narvik and Petsamo, as well as coastal security duties under the command of Seekommandant Hammerfest. It too was seconded to Landung Einsatzstab Polarküste in September 1944, evacuating personnel and equipment from northern Finland and Lapland. Used for crossings of Altafjord and Kvaenangenfjord, MFPs were also added as anti-aircraft protection for *Tirpitz* in Altafjord. The remainder of the war saw the flotilla involved in a steady stream of evacuation missions.

Depot ship for the 7th R-Flotilla, SS *Weser*, approaches the quay in Kirkenes for bunkering in 1943. (Finnmark Fylkesbibliotek)

9th L-Flotilla

Formed in Narvik in June 1944, between September that year and March 1945, the flotilla took part in evacuations from the northern Finland and Lapland region under the control of Landung Einsatzstab

Polarküste. It subsequently continued to be used for short-distance coastal transport operations between Petsamo and Narvik.

21st L-Flotilla

Formed on 1 April 1942 in Swinemünde, two groups of MFPs were stationed between May and June 1942 in Kirkenes as auxiliary security vessels, transport craft and artillery carriers. They were due to take part in the amphibious attack on the Fischer Peninsula (Operation *Wiesengrund*) which was repeatedly postponed until finally cancelled in 1944. Between June and August 1942, the flotilla was deployed to bombard enemy positions on the Fischer Peninsula, returning to Germany at the beginning of 1943.

22nd L-Flotilla

Also formed in Swinemünde in September 1942, the 22nd L-Flotilla was moved to Kirkenes during December to relieve the 21st L-Flotilla. In April 1943, parts of the flotilla moved to Hammerfest, some later being used for anti-aircraft protection in the Altafjord. In June 1944, the flotilla was renamed the 6th L-Flotilla and its headquarters moved to Hammerfest.

23rd L-Flotilla

Formed on 1 October 1942 in Swinemünde, 23rd L-Flotilla moved to Kirkenes in April 1943. Used for minelaying and transport duties, the flotilla was also employed against the Soviet beachhead on the south-east coast of the Varanger Peninsula on 28 March 1944. In June 1944, the flotilla was renamed the 5th L-Flotilla.

F224 of the 21st L-Flotilla carrying Gebirgsjäger in northern Norway. (Author Collection)

COMBAT AND ANALYSIS

THE FLEET IN COMBAT

1940

Generaladmiral Hermann Boehm flew into Oslo on the afternoon of 10 April as commander of all German naval forces in Norway, his subordinates, Konteradmiral Otto Schenk and Admiral Otto von Schrader, also arriving that day as Admirals South and West, respectively. The German invasion of Norway was barely one day old and, though Germany would prevail, weeks of difficult fighting lay ahead. Narvik in particular saw heavy German casualties, including ten Kriegsmarine destroyers sunk by the Royal Navy.

Boehm had been specifically chosen by Grossadmiral Raeder as the senior Kriegsmarine officer for Norway due to what he later described as his 'firm yet understanding manner', which Raeder hoped would foster a conciliatory relationship between the Kriegsmarine and the Norwegian authorities. This would place Boehm at odds with the German commissioner appointed to Norway, Reichskommissar Josef Terboven, who arrived on 24 April. Terboven's authority was officially limited to civilian affairs, but he negotiated terms with the SS which enabled cooperation between him, the *Sicherheitsdienst* (SD, the SS Security Service) and *Geheime Staatspolizei* (Gestapo). Boehm frequently clashed with Terboven over the latter's increasingly harsh treatment of the Norwegian population, but to no avail.

Even before Norwegian capitulation on 10 June, the immediate Kriegsmarine priority was the seizure of local vessels suitable either as transport ships to sustain the invasion or conversion to security vessels. Requests for minesweeping, patrol and anti-submarine units could not be met, as the Kriegsmarine was already stretched to its limit. The first year of Kriegsmarine activity within Norway comprised establishing firm German control over ports and harbours in the face of, at best, Norwegian indifference or, at worst, outright hostility. Minesweeping and anti-submarine missions took precedence as the Royal Navy made its underwater presence felt along the eastern extremities of the North Sea.

Ashore, ports and harbours were fortified and naval flak and artillery units moved into position as workers from Organization Todt expanded existing Norwegian infrastructure to support future capital ship and U-boat operations. Norway provided a strategic springboard into the North Atlantic, where the convoy war raged, and would also feature in Hitler's future planes to invade the Soviet Union, on which he had already decided by the end of the year.

1941

At 0700hrs on 4 March, Seekommandant Narvik reported by telex the sighting of three eastbound British destroyers from the Skrova lighthouse. The ships were part of 6th Destroyer Flotilla, escorting the attack force of commandos and Royal Engineers making a surprise landing on the Lofoten Islands. The primary task of Operation *Claymore* was destruction of fish oil factories and storage tanks in four Lofoten ports, the oil an important component in the manufacture of glycerine for the German armaments industry. The capture of enemy personnel, collaborators and intelligence material, and destruction of enemy shipping, were also part of *Claymore*'s purpose; the first of 12 major Allied raids on Norwegian soil – four of them in 1941 alone.

Though a Luftwaffe weather flight had already detected the incoming ships and the coastal alert status raised to 'increased watchfulness', *Claymore* was a complete success. Eight merchant ships were sunk during the attack, including the 5,532-GRT SS *'Hamburg'*, the first fully freezer-equipped fishing factory ship. During the previous month, Boehm had already urged Terboven not to station this modern vessel in Svolvær in the Lofoten Islands following espionage reports but had been rebuffed. Two hundred and twenty-eight prisoners were taken back to Britain, along with nearly 300 Norwegian volunteers.

A further coup for the Royal Navy was the sinking of the 376-ton armed trawler *NN04 'Krebs'* of Narvik's Hafenschutzflottille near one of the commando landing zones on Svolvær. Lead destroyer HMS *Somali* opened fire on the woefully outgunned *Krebs* at a range of just under two miles, return fire causing no damage while the trawler was battered into submission. *Krebs*' wheelhouse took a direct hit, which killed the captain – Leutnant zur See Hans Kapfinger – and several crew. The trawler was soon incapacitated and stranded on a low rocky islet, where most survivors abandoned ship.

Somali departed to supervise troop landings, returning hours later after *Krebs* had refloated on a rising tide. A boarding party secured a naval grid map, personal papers and documents and two Enigma rotors from a locked cupboard, as well as five wounded Germans, two of them severely injured. *Somali* then sank *Krebs* with depth charges and shellfire, and Bletchley Park later made good use of the Enigma rotors, cypher material for February and plugboard settings that had been among the valuable haul.

On 18 March, in conference with Raeder, Hitler ordered Norwegian coastal defence strengthened by Army coastal artillery. Batteries of 30.5cm guns, 21cm mortars and torpedoes were directed to Narvik, a 28cm railway gun to be used during the establishment period for the new batteries. Raeder also strongly urged greater Luftwaffe commitment to deter enemy warships.

A naval artillery Matrosenobergefreiter stands guard at one of *Marine Küsten Batterie* (Naval Coastal Battery) 4./517's four 24cm SKL/40 main guns at Mestersand. The four guns and two torpedo batteries of MAA 517 were under the command of *Der Kommandant der Seeverteidigung von Kirkenes* (Commander of Kirkenes Naval Defence). (Finnmark Fylkesbibliotek)

Norway's geography posed significant problems for German security forces, both ashore and at sea. The Kriegsmarine continually struggled to gather sufficient vessels as, though Norway provided an excellent strategic springboard into the Atlantic, the primary German concern was defensive. Naval forces frequently worked in conjunction with Wehrmacht and SS intelligence to combat Norwegian resistance and an increasing tempo of Allied infiltration and exfiltration. A case in point was on 31 March, when, in cooperation with Trondheim's SD commander, Obersturmführer Julius Nielsen, eight Englishmen were arrested after their vessel was stopped by *V5503 'Zick'* while attempting to depart for England.

Kriegsmarine engineers worked extensively to fortify the major ports and harbours. Existing Norwegian naval infrastructure was expanded, with floating docks, fuel depots, repair workshops and personnel accommodation, all protected by naval flak batteries.

Before June 1941, German destroyers had only entered Norwegian bases while acting as escort for major ships preparing to break from the North Sea into the Atlantic Ocean. They had successfully escorted *Bismarck* and *Prinz Eugen* at the outset of the ill-fated Operation *Rheinübung* during May, and the heavy cruiser *Lützow* in June, though the latter's attempted foray was curtailed by an RAF Beaufort torpedo that hit the cruiser and forced a return to Germany for six months of repairs.

Since the destruction of battleship *Bismarck* on 27 May, Hitler fixated on the resulting loss of prestige and forbade any more capital ship sorties into the Atlantic. He insisted that major Kriegsmarine units take no unnecessary risks, severely restricting their movements and the ability of them to enter action unless specifically released to do so by his personal orders. In one stroke he neutered the Kriegsmarine's major surface forces.

With the launch of Operation *Barbarossa* in June, five serviceable ships of Kapitän zur See Alfred Schulze-Hinrichs' 6th Destroyer Flotilla were ordered to the Arctic, arriving in Kirkenes on 10 July. Anchored in the fjord around the island of Renøy, Hinrichs was briefed by Konteradmiral Schenk, Generaloberst Eduard Dietl and General Stumpff (commander of Luftflotte 5) on the destroyers' forthcoming role supporting the German offensive.

Operation *Silverfox* (*Silberfuchs*) had been launched by Dietl's Alpine Corps (*Gebirgskorps Norwegen*) and Finnish troops to secure Murmansk. The portion of the offensive assaulting from Petsamo directly towards Murmansk was codenamed *Platinum Fox* (*Platinfuchs*). The Kriegsmarine had repeatedly emphasized the importance of capturing Murmansk, believing that the longer it remained unoccupied the greater incentive it offered to Britain to obtain a foothold there, both for access to the Atlantic and the feared landing of British troops that would stiffen resistance and divert German reinforcements from other fronts.

Delayed by awaiting Finnish cooperation, *Silberfuchs* had launched on 29 June. Fighting over some of the most inhospitable terrain on Earth, the advance soon stalled in the face of stubborn Soviet resistance. Soviet marines were also landed by destroyers behind the German lines, contributing shore bombardment to the confused fighting as German troops were compelled to halt and deal with this and other smaller landings. Furthermore, the German troops of *Platinfuchs* required supply by sea, a route that soon came under attack by freshly deployed Royal Navy submarines and elements of the Soviet Northern Fleet. Reinforcing troops faced a tortuous journey, travelling by sea to Kristiansand, by rail to Trondheim and then being re-embarked on transports that had carried their equipment for the remaining journey north. *Platinfuchs* devolved into trench warfare along the line of the Liza River, halfway between Petsamo and Murmansk, seeing little movement until 1944.

To support the flagging ground battle, the destroyers of the *6th Zerstörerflottille* (Destroyer Flotilla) immediately launched their own offensive along the Kola coast, though they were under severe constraints. The entrances to Kola and Motovski bays were heavily mined, and with neither R-boat nor Luftwaffe support available in the area, operations by destroyers and U-boats were

OPERATION *SILVER FOX*

In June 1941, German and Finnish forces launched Operation *Silberfuchs* (Silver Fox) to attack Murmansk from two directions. The assault from Finnish Petsamo directly towards the port of Murmansk was codenamed *Platinfuchs* (Platinum Fox), launched on 29 June. Gebirgs Korps Nowegen under the command of Generalleutnant Eduard Dietl, consisting of the German 2nd and 3rd Gebirgs Divisions as well as the Finnish Ivalo Border Guard Battalion, advanced against units of the Soviet 14th Army and were soon bogged down against a fiercely resistant and motivated defence.

In September, elements of 6th Gebirgs Division were sent as reinforcement to Dietl's corps, but suffered severe casualties. Troops transports *Bahia Laura* and *Donau II* were both torpedoed and sunk by the British submarine HMS *Trident* at position 70.27 N, 21.55 E, with 447 men killed. In total, 1,122 survivors were rescued by escorting destroyers *Hans Lody* and *Karl Galster*, R153, V6111 *'Franke'*, V6113 *'Gote'* and Norwegian ship *Midnatsol*. Escorting UJ178, UJ176 and UJ177 dropped 56 depth charges over the following two hours, but *Trident* escaped.

Further loss was avoided when destroyer-sized gunnery training ship *Bremse* was used as convoy escort for troopships *Trautenfels* and *Barcelona* along with *V6103 'Nordlicht'*, UJ1701 and R162. Carrying 1,500 men of the 6th Gebirgs Division from Tromsø to Kirkenes, the convoy was intercepted by British cruisers HMS *Nigeria* and *Aurora* near the island of Magerøya, whereupon *Bremse* attacked, sacrificing itself as the troopships escaped. The presence of naval and army coastal artillery batteries had prevented neither Royal Navy attack.

MKB 18./971 Melkøya
MKB 1./514 Hammerfest
HKB 19./971
Skippernes
Bahia Laura &
Donau II sunk
here
Bremse sunk here
MKB 2./513 Vadsø
HKB 3./478
Kvalneset (Vadsø)
HKB 564 Vardø
MKB 4./513
Vadsø
Hammerfest
HBK 5./971 Børselvnes
HKB 32./971
Oksfjord
HBK 4./971 Bratholmen
HKB 8./Vagsnes
HBK 6./971 Kistrand
HKB 37./971 Nordstrømmen
HKB 37./971 Rakkenes
HKB 36./971 Storeng
Tromsø
Alta
HKB 17./971 Kvalsund
MKB 3./514 Store Korsnes
HKB 999 Høibukten
Kirkenes

restricted to the sea area between the two bays, aimed to prevent or at least impede the Soviet supply route from Archangelsk to Murmansk, Murmansk to Litsa Bay, and Archangelsk to Kandalaksha.

The first destroyer sortie began on 12 July, sinking two small military vessels travelling in convoy but having no appreciable effect on the fighting ashore. Under serious threat from aircraft, they ultimately achieved little and would have been better used in providing direct artillery support to the Wehrmacht troops ashore. Soviet destroyers frequently landed troops, their German counterparts making no serious efforts to intercept them.

A second destroyer sortie begun on 22 July ended with the destruction of Soviet survey ship *Meridian* by gunfire from the destroyer *Hermann Schoemann*. *Meridian* had been evacuating women and children from lighthouse attendant families for return to Archangelsk, and 46 of the 63 people aboard were killed. A third offensive sweep took place on 9 August by *Z10 'Hans Lody'*, *Z4 'Richard Beitzen'* (on loan from the 5th Flotilla) and *Z16 'Friedrich Eckholdt'*, as both *Z20 'Karl Galster'* and *Z7 'Hermann Schoemann'* were elsewhere engaged on convoy escort duties. The destroyers sank the converted trawler *SKR12 'Tuman'* that was patrolling the entrance to the Kola Inlet. Soviet coastal artillery opened fire, forcing Hinrichs to move further offshore, where they were dogged by repeated air attack. While Hinrichs aboard Z10 returned to Kirkenes, both Z4 and Z16 were despatched to Narvik for shipyard overhaul. However, a further attack caused enough damage to Z4 that it had to be sent back to Germany for a complete refit. The remaining destroyers were thereafter used predominantly for escort work as German coastal convoys came under increasing pressure.

Though the Red Banner Northern Fleet vastly outnumbered German regional strength, and included 15 submarines, it was Royal Navy submarines that made their presence felt most strongly during August. Both HMS *Trident* and *Tigris* had been sent to operate from the Soviet naval base at Polyarny. During its inaugural patrol, *Trident* had already damaged transport ship *Levante* with gunfire and sunk transport *Ostpreussen*, causing SKL to record within its war diary that 'the lack of submarine hunters is now having an impact'.

Hinrichs' flotilla was soon reduced to three after mechanical damage forced *Schoemann* back to Germany, an intended replacement running aground while travelling north and also requiring extensive repair.

Both Z10 (as Hinrichs' flagship) and Z20 were part of the escort for a convoy of four merchant ships bound from Tromsø to Kirkenes on 30 August when HMS *Trident* torpedoed and sank the 8,561-GRT SS *Bahia Laura* and 2,931-GRT SS *Donau II*, the two ships carrying 1,598 soldiers and 78 crew between them. Due to fine weather and effective rescue, 1,334 survivors were later put ashore. Retaliatory depth charging caused minor damage aboard *Trident*.

Meanwhile, much against Dönitz's advice, several U-boats were despatched from Germany to the polar seas to support the ground attack against Murmansk by intercepting enemy military and merchant shipping. The Type

VIICs U81 and U652 arrived first, while U451 and U566 were scheduled to leave Trondheim for the Arctic on 23 July. Oberleutnant zur See Georg-Werner Fraatz's U652 sailed from Kiel to Horten on 19 June. The boat was administratively attached to Kiel's 3rd U-boat Flotilla but beneath the command umbrella of Kommandierender Admiral Norwegen. Fraatz and his crew docked in Bøkfjorden in Finnmark on 22 July. There, within the 23km-long fjord, U652 moored at the small town of Kirkenes. The Kriegsmarine had designated Kirkenes as its operational centre on the northern Arctic coast. The large depot ship MV *Black Watch*, commissioned into service there during August 1940, was later joined by MV *Stella Polaris* as the U-boat presence increased.

Dönitz fumed at what he perceived as a waste of resources as Allied convoys carrying supplies to Russia had not yet started. He feared that these U-boats would simply roam the empty seas while they would be better used in the Atlantic convoy war. Not until 6 August would any of the Arctic boats draw blood, when Fraatz sank 558-ton Russian ASW trawler RT70 7 miles off Cape Teriberka with a single G7e torpedo.

Even less suited to the Arctic water were *Schnellboote* (fast attack craft) of the 8th S-Flotilla placed under Boehm's operational control in October. Newly commissioned S42, S44, S45 and S46 travelled from Kiel in November, motoring first to Bergen, from where they were taken under tow to spare the S-boats' engines. The flotilla and tender *Adolf Lüderitz* arrived in Trondheim on 4 December. There they were joined by the depot ship *Tanga*, also headed to Kirkenes to act as headquarters ship while transporting ammunition and supplies for the S-boats. Supporting units also sailed to Norway: freighter *Larsen* to Trondheim, where it underwent conversion to a workshop ship, and steamer *Herösand* arriving for transformation to torpedo arsenal and balancing station. *Tanga* sailed in company with destroyers despatched to reinforce the Arctic front, while the S-boats were frequently delayed by bad weather, arriving in Tromsø on 15 December under escort by destroyers Z25 and Z27.

On Boxing Day, British commandoes attacked the Lofoten Islands as part of Operation *Anklet*, the next day more commandoes landing at Vågsøy in Operation *Archery*. Local Kriegsmarine forces were immediately placed on high alert and ordered to intercept supporting British naval units. At 1206hrs, the 8th Z-Flotilla and 8th S-Flotilla received orders to patrol west of the Lofoten Islands. The S-boats were not underway until four hours later, by which time enemy contact was thought unlikely and the flotilla was recalled. The result of their commitment was S45 scraping the shallow fjord bottom and sustaining enough damage to necessitate shipyard work in Harstad. The following day, after British landings in Vågsøy, Boehm posted the 8th S-Flotilla

U622 takes on torpedoes from the torpedo arsenal at Askøy near Bergen. U622 mounted four Arctic war patrols while part of the 11th and 13th U-boat Flotillas but was sunk quayside in Trondheim during a raid by 45 B17 bombers of the Eighth Air Force, USSAF, on 24 July 1943. This was the first day that American bombers attacked targets in Norway. (Author Collection)

to Narvik in readiness for potential action (the Narvik designation granted by Hitler in recognition of the April 1940 battles). S42, S44 and S46 arrived in Narvik with their tender on 28 December, S42 and S44 colliding during their first alert, lowering the flotilla's fully operational strength to only two boats.

Meanwhile, Hinrichs' 6th Destroyer Flotilla's active strength was whittled down by mechanical and personnel problems until, at the beginning of September, none were operative. Instead, destroyer-sized gunnery training ship *Bremse*, under the command of Korvettenkapitän Hermann von Brosy-Steinberg, was used as convoy escort and on 7 September was escorting troopships *Trautenfels* and *Barcelona* near Mageröy-Fjord, along with *V6103 'Nordlicht'*, submarine chaser UJ1701 and R162. The ships were carrying 1,500 men of the 6th Gebirgs Division from Tromsø to Kirkenes but was intercepted by British cruisers HMS *Nigeria* and *Aurora* near the island of Magerøya. Steinberg reported enemy ships sighted at 0323hrs and immediately ordered *Bremse* to close the attackers to draw them away from the transports. Hopelessly outgunned, *Bremse* was hammered by withering close-range fire and sunk. Following the British withdrawal, V6103 and R162 pulled 37 surviving crew from the water, and five corpses including the captain.

With a dearth of escort vessels and slim Luftwaffe availability made worse by the approach of winter, SKL deemed troop transports unable to proceed east of North Cape. Supply steamers could do so only at very great risk until Murmansk was occupied; ironically only plausible with the troop reinforcement and supply now being denied.

By December, the last of the 6th Flotilla's destroyers was back in Germany for refit, replaced by the incoming 8th (Narvik) Destroyer Flotilla; its first two ships, Z24 and Z26, reaching Tromsø in late November. In the meantime, Allied Arctic convoys had begun during August, travelling to Archangelsk with minimal interference. By 20 December, 47 ships had successfully reached Archangelsk in six convoys, only a single ship forced to return to Iceland after suffering ice damage.

Dönitz elected to use new combat U-boats from Germany for Arctic patrols, Kapitänleutnant Ernst Vogelsang's U132 mounting the longest Arctic mission thus far, 45 days beginning in September and proving the most successful, sinking unescorted 3,487-ton steamer *Argun* and 608-ton naval trawler *RT8 'Seld'*.

During October 1941, the post of Admiral Nordmeer was established, Admiral Hubert Schmundt occupying the position until August 1942 and responsible for U-boat deployment within a central band of the Arctic Ocean from his headquarters aboard *Tanga* in Kirkenes, the remainder remaining under

Schnellboote moored alongside their depot ship in Kirkenes. S-boats were highly unsuited to both Arctic conditions and the task of convoy escort for which they were regularly used. (Naval History and Heritage Command)

Boehm's control, in a confusing arrangement. Reinforcement of the Arctic U-boat presence to at least nine boats had been requested by Boehm, but denied, much to Dönitz's relief as he faced the prospect of opening a new front against the United States with yet more U-boats taken away from the Atlantic. Boehm also objected to the assignment of only new, inexperienced U-boats, arguing that veteran U-boat commanders were required in such a challenging environment. Though persuaded to allow U-boats to remain with Boehm for more than one patrol, Dönitz steadfastly refused to remove veterans from the Atlantic.

During November, Raeder recommended that the now operational *Tirpitz* be moved from the Baltic to Trondheim, as Hitler fixated on a potential British landing in Norway. There, *Tirpitz* could threaten the flank of enemy operations against the northern Norwegian coast while attacking White Sea convoys and bombarding land installations, necessitating heavy enemy forces be held to counter *Tirpitz*. The battleship arrived in Trondheim during

Räumboote off the Norwegian coast. (Naval History and Heritage Command)

GUNNERY TRAINING SHIP *BREMSE* UNDER ATTACK

The advent of the artillery training ship *Bremse* – commissioned in 1931 – was intended to help drill gunnery personnel of the new Kriegsmarine as part of the drive to expand the navy and to replace older ships and naval weaponry with updated models. It was also used as a testbed for diesel engines which were later installed in the new-build Panzerschiff *Deutschland*.

Bremse took part in Operation *Weserübung*, and with a lack of destroyers available for convoy escort duty due to maintenance issues in the Arctic, the destroyer-sized *Bremse* – under the command of Korvettenkapitän Hermann von Brosy-Steinberg – was used as convoy escort. It survived an attack by British Albacore bombers during July 1941, and on 7 September was shepherding troopships north to reinforce the attack towards Murmansk. *Bremse* was escorting troopships *Trautenfels* and *Barcelona* near Mageröy-Fjord, alongside the patrol boat *V6103 'Nordlicht'*, submarine hunter UJ1701 and motor minesweeper R162. The troopships were carrying 1,500 men of the 6th Gebirgs Division from Tromsø to Kirkenes.

Thanks to the deciphering of German Enigma signals, Rear Admiral Philip Vian's Force K that had covered an Allied attack on Spitzbergen was alerted to the likelihood of the German convoy expected to reach Hammerfjord shortly. Detaching two cruisers – his flagship HMS *Nigeria* and HMS *Aurora* – Vian decided to approach the Norwegian coast, covered by bad weather. Near the island of Magerøya, radar contact was made with the convoy. Aboard *Bremse*, Steinberg reported enemy ships sighted at 0323hrs, appearing between himself and the convoy body. He immediately ordered *Bremse* to lay smoke and close the attackers to draw them away from the transports. Hopelessly outgunned, *Bremse* was hammered by withering close-range fire and sank. Following the British withdrawal, V6103 and R162 pulled 37 surviving crew from the water, and five corpses including the captain.

January, moving to Fættenfjord under destroyer escort, mooring cliffside to minimize danger from air attack. There, camouflaged by netting and tree branches and protected by smoke screen generators, torpedo nets and extra anti-aircraft guns established ashore, the great ship waited. Its presence revealed by Norwegian resistance fighters, RAF Bomber Command made two attempts in March and April 1942 to attack *Tirpitz*, achieving no success for the loss of 12 aircraft.

On 25 December 1941, SKL recorded reports from the Finnish envoy to Washington of a British–American–Norwegian landing being prepared for northern Norway. Though SKL notified both MGK Nord Carls and Boehm of the information, they advised that they considered such a plan 'unlikely'. However, they tacitly acknowledged that such a landing that complemented and took advantage of Russian winter successes to the east was not out of the question. The idea of hampering German Arctic naval operations and drawing German troops from the Eastern Front would no doubt be tempting, but beyond current capabilities. Therefore, they conceded that it was not inconceivable for planning of a localized invasion for the purpose of obtaining a foothold in northern Norway to be underway, a rumour that found wide circulation within Wehrmacht units.

Hitler's notable fixation with this perceived Allied threat was not without justification. Winston Churchill lobbied consistently for an amphibious assault and occupation of the Norwegian coast. He reasoned that it was a way of attacking the Reich's 'soft underbelly', providing forward bomber bases and a launch ramp for an invasion of Germany. Despite being opposed by all senior Allied commanders, Stalin fuelled Churchill's dream by requesting in July 1941 the despatch of '25 to 30 divisions' to Archangel. Though clearly a fanciful idea, Churchill repeatedly returned to the idea of landings in Trondheim and subsequent occupation of Norway. His final memorandum in May 1942, headed 'Operation *Jupiter*', urged this as an alternative to plans percolating for an attack on France but it was finally refused by the Allied Joint Chiefs of Staff.

Nonetheless, as part of Allied deception ahead of the Normandy landings, Operation *Tindall* fabricated a British Fourth Army based in Scotland, with its headquarters at Edinburgh Castle. The illusion was sustained with fake radio traffic and information fed through captured Abwehr agents who had been turned, reinforced by stepped-up British commando raids in Norway and increased naval activity in the northern North Sea. Because the Luftwaffe could not reliably reconnoitre the area, the ruse required no physical presence. By late spring 1944, it had tied down 13 Wehrmacht divisions in Norway; Operation *Fortitude North* then carried the fiction further into 1944, again supported by commando attacks on Norwegian targets.

1942

On 5 January, Generaladmiral Rolf Carls (MGK Nord) provided SKL with a complete inventory of all minesweepers, R-boats and Vorpostenboote under his command, starkly illustrating that it was no longer possible to cede further units to other theatres of operation without completely jeopardizing Norwegian naval security. However, raw materials, building yards and manpower remained insufficient within Germany to enable the necessary expansion of its security forces. The Kriegsmarine was therefore compelled to prioritize allocation of whatever forces were available to meet the most urgent need as the war expanded far beyond German capabilities.

This was reflected in Dönitz resentfully assigning an unnecessarily large number of U-boats to Norway despite his strongest objections. Increasingly concerned about a possible Allied landing, Hitler had proclaimed Norway as the Reich's 'zone of destiny' in conference with naval chiefs on 22 January, demanding 'unconditional obedience' to all his wishes regarding defence of this region.

This diversion of U-boat strength could not have come at a worse time for Dönitz. He had committed five Type IX long-range boats to the initial attack on the United States (Operation *Paukenschlag*), followed by a second wave and a third headed to the Caribbean (Operation *Neuland*). With all long-range boats assigned, he turned to available Type VIICs and also threw them against the woefully unprepared Americans. Despite spectacular success, the window of opportunity for maximum impact versus minimal risk had passed by May 1942, the United States Navy having finally learnt to accept British recommendations of convoying merchant traffic, as the main Allied navies began closer effective coordination.

The 8th S-Flotilla was ordered during January to proceed in company with the 8th Destroyer Flotilla to Vardø, the easternmost town in Norway, where the S-boats would be based. Tender *Adolf Lüderitz* began the voyage on the afternoon of 3 January, S44 and S46 reaching Vardø on 6 January, where they were laid up for two days for maintenance and then forced to remain in harbour by high winds sweeping across the barren Varanger Peninsula. A high sea ran directly into the unsheltered harbour and it quickly became apparent that, although the port was ice-free all year round due to the North Atlantic drift, it was totally unsuitable as a flotilla base. Additionally, they attracted the attention of Russian bombers which, though relatively ineffectual, added to an already moribund atmosphere amongst the S-boat men. On 12 January, they relocated to the port of Vadsø on the southern coast of the Varanger Peninsula and more sheltered from the elements, as evidenced by birch forests that dominated the surrounding countryside.

Elsewhere in Norway, the elderly S15 was despatched from Bergen in company with torpedo boat *V5501 'Zick'* to hunt for the cruiser HMS *Sheffield* and destroyers HMS *Inglefield* and *Intrepid* that had shelled the town of Florø as part of the raiding Operation *Kitbag II*, again destroying fish-oil processing plants. The German search was unsuccessful.

By this stage, MGK Nord requested the permanent stationing of 12 S-boats within the Arctic Circle, a request refused on the grounds that there simply were not enough S-boats to fulfil demand. Carls insisted that they were necessary for an extensive minelaying programme planned by Boehm that would include six offensive minefields off Kola Bay; three to be laid by destroyers, three by S-boats.

By 28 January, the sea at Vadsø had frozen over and the 8th S-Flotilla was forced to relocate once more, this time to Semske Fjord near Kirkenes. Two fruitless torpedo operations had been mounted in the perpetual darkness of the polar winter, neither sighting any enemy units. Reinforcing failure, SKL recommended that the 1st S-Flotilla be sent to Norway while 8th S-Flotilla was to be expanded to eight boats. Lying completely idle until 15 March, the first mission was minelaying off the Arctic coast, which was abandoned after four hours in storm conditions. Four boats successfully escorted minelayer *Ulm* on 19 March, the 'Bantos A' minefield being sown near Helnes Lighthouse on the North Cape. Meanwhile, on 15 February, the decision was made not to divert the 1st S-Flotilla but rather Kapitänleutnant Albrecht Obermaier's 6th S-Flotilla, engaged at that time in Channel operations. Obermaier's unit was withdrawn from the battle and ordered to transfer with tender *Tsingtau* to the Lofoten–Narvik area. Harstad was, at first, considered the optimal flotilla berth until Commanding Admiral Norway designated the port at Svolvær on Austvågøya Island as flotilla base. Obermaier's flotilla was ordered to remain on constant alert, anchorages changing periodically to diminish the chance of enemy interference.

In Kirkenes, 6th S-Flotilla commander, Kapitänleutnant Georg Christiansen, repeatedly reported the unsuitability of S-boats within the Arctic Circle. What few missions they had been able to sail had been completely ineffectual, not a single torpedo fired or mine laid as the boats wrestled with conditions beyond their capabilities. Their use as convoy escorts and harbour protection harkened back to the war's early days, when the role of the fast attack craft was little understood. The wear and tear on engine parts and crews far outweighed what meagre use they were in tasks far better suited to converted trawlers of the Vorpostenboot flotillas and U-Boot Jäger. Common sense finally prevailed and Admiral Nordmeer relented, though SKL maintained that the boats of 6th S-Flotilla remain where they were as a defensive weapon against the spectre of Allied invasion.

Marinegruppenkommando Nord was authorized to split the flotilla, five boats being transferred to Semske Fjord to take over the post left by the departing 8th S-Flotilla. They also swapped tenders, as the *Adolf Lüderitz* was equipped with powerful radio gear needed as a repeat station for short-wave traffic from Arctic U-boats until an equivalent radio station could be built ashore.

During early February, battleships *Scharnhorst* and *Gneisenau* and heavy cruiser *Prinz Eugen* had made their spectacular 'Channel dash' (Operation

Cerberus) from Brest to Germany before planned deployment in Norway to bolster defence against the phantom British invasion. However, only one of the trio – *Prinz Eugen* – was deployed to Norway, *Scharnhorst* having suffered mine damage during *Cerberus*, which would keep the ship in Kiel until July. *Gneisenau* had also struck a mine, though repairs were completed by 26 February. In Kiel, the ship was attacked by the RAF; one bomb exploded in the forward ammunition magazine and caused serious damage and casualties. Ultimately it was never repaired.

On 21 February, *Admiral Scheer*, *Prinz Eugen* and escorting destroyers of the 6th Flotilla returning to Norway – *Z4 'Richard Beitzen'*, *Z5 'Paul Jakobi'*, *Z7 'Hermann Schoemann'*, *Z14 'Friedrich Ihn'* and *Z25* – left Germany. Two days later, HMS *Trident* torpedoed *Prinz Eugen*, killing 50 men and causing extensive damage requiring shipyard repairs until October. Meanwhile, *Admiral Scheer* moored near Trondheim.

Though *Prinz Eugen* was forced away from Norway, heavy cruiser *Admiral Hipper* transferred to Trondheim during March under destroyer and torpedo boat escort, and in May heavy cruiser *Lützow* sailed from Swinemünde to join

S44 AND S46 ENTER VARDØ, A NEW FLOTILLA BASE

At the beginning of 1942, instructions were given for the 8th S-Flotilla to proceed in company with the 8th Destroyer Flotilla, to Vardø, the easternmost town in Norway. This was to be the S-boats' Arctic base. Tender *Adolf Lüderitz* began the voyage on the afternoon of 3 January, as those S-boats that were operational were already sailing from Tromsø to Honningsvåg and then onwards the following morning. S44 and S46 reached Vardø in Finnmark on 6 January, laid up for two days for maintenance and were then forced to remain in harbour by high winds sweeping across the barren Varanger Peninsula. A high sea ran directly into the unsheltered harbour and it quickly became apparent that, although the port was ice-free all year round due to the North Atlantic drift, it was totally unsuitable as a flotilla base. They also attracted the attention of Russian bombers which, though relatively ineffectual, added to an already moribund atmosphere amongst the S-boat men. On 12 January, they relocated to the port of Vadsø, on the southern coast of the Varanger Peninsula and more sheltered from the elements, as evidenced by birch forests that dominated the surrounding countryside.

Marinegruppenkommando Nord (Generaladmiral Carls) had requested the permanent stationing of 12 S-boats within the Arctic Circle, a request refused on the grounds that there simply were not enough S-boats available. Carls' justification remained that, even if hampered by the kind of ice that inhibited peacetime shipping, merchant vessels laden with supplies for Russia could still pass through the White Sea. An extensive minelaying programme was planned by Commanding Admiral Norway (Generaladmiral Boehm) that included six offensive minefields off Kola Bay: three to be laid by destroyers, three by S-boats.

Conditions aboard the boats at sea were barely tolerable; flak weapons, depth charges and mine rails all totally iced over and becoming unserviceable, while men were forced to frequently change watches in the subzero temperatures. Aboard the tender *Adolf Lüderitz*, things were at least comfortable, but the interminable darkness and lack of diversions ashore when off duty did little to improve spirits. Even their diet began to suffer as supplies from Germany began to dry up and convoys bringing fresh produce were increasingly intercepted by the British. Bartering fresh fish locally in exchange for Schnapps at least kept a portion of their menu away from reconstituted dried rations, but a lack of fruit and vegetables contributed to a general decline in crew health.

Tirpitz and *Admiral Scheer* in preparation for Norwegian operations. *Lützow* became the flagship of Vizeadmiral Oskar Kummetz, Commander of Cruisers (B.d.K.). The heavy ships faced severe fuel shortages. Romanian production was virtually Germany's only source and imports had rapidly declined, fulfilling only one-tenth of naval requirements. All operations by major units were discontinued.

Destroyers of Kapitän zur See Gottfried Pönitz's 8th (Narvik) Destroyer Flotilla had replaced Hinrichs' flotilla in Kirkenes. During December, they had made a sweep off the Murman coast, unsuccessfully skirmishing with two British minesweepers.

On 5 March, Luftwaffe reconnaissance spotted incoming convoy PQ12, and, to join four U-boats already at sea, Hitler authorized *Tirpitz* to intercept in Operation *Sportpalast*. Destroyers *Z14 'Friedrich Ihn'*, *Z5 'Paul Jacobi'*, *Z7 'Hermann Schoemann'* and *Z25* – as well as torpedo boat T5 and T12 – escorted the battleship into action. However, *Tirpitz* failed to find the convoy due to faulty Luftwaffe coordinates. *Tirpitz* narrowly missed convoy QP8 which had left Murmansk, but straggling 2,815-GRT Soviet timber carrier SS *Izhora* was found and shelled by *'Friedrich Ihn'*, eventually being finished off with depth charges dropped nearby. Plain text distress signals giving *Tirpitz*'s coordinates were received by ships of PQ12 and QP8, and the convoys were diverted on Admiralty orders. Instead, the Home Fleet was despatched to attack the battleship, which was targeted by Albacore torpedo aircraft from HMS *Victorious*. *Tirpitz* successfully combed the tracks of the incoming torpedoes and escaped, two Albacores being shot down. Three KG 30 Ju88s attempted to bomb the carrier in return, narrowly missing with dive-bombing attacks.

Tirpitz's deployment against PQ12 used 8,230 metric tons of fuel oil, which took the Kriegsmarine three months to recoup. Such critically low fuel stocks curtailed destroyer operations, the next mission launched unsuccessfully during April, drawing harsh criticism of the way it was carried out contrary to directions from Admiral Nordmeer and MGK Nord. Boehm continued to request additional Vorpostenboote, U-Jäger and minesweepers, but was denied due to the lack of vessels. Instead, he was urged to use existing craft of the various Hafenschutzflottillen for these expanded duties. During the first months of 1942, both German and Soviet surface craft successfully laid elaborate and dense minefields along the polar coast, the former to protect vulnerable supply convoys from Soviet and British submarines. Throughout the first six months of 1942, 872 freighters carrying 2,608,057 tons of supplies successfully shuttled between Narvik and Kirkenes.

Lützow at sea, 1942. *Lützow* began life as the Panzerschiffe *Deutschland*, renamed after its return from its first and only sortie to the Atlantic. (Naval History and Heritage Command)

In Berlin, the requested scale of Norwegian coastal security was continually raised. Following the British raid on Saint-Nazaire, SKL ordered Trondheim Fjord 'hermetically sealed' to protect the major warships. However, Boehm then requested the allocation of further antiaircraft batteries with crews, depth-charge throwers, floating net barrages and a UJ-flotilla consisting of 12 vessels to guarantee effectiveness of the net barrages.

Offensively, results were poor. Of four U-boats lying in wait for PQ13 or outbound QP9, U655 was rammed and sunk by escorting minesweeper HMS *Sharpshooter*, south-east of Bear Island. Two ships from PQ13 were torpedoed by U-boats and Pönitz also took destroyers Z24, Z25 and Z26 into action against the convoy. They found and sank straggling 6,097-GRT Panamanian freighter SS *Bateau*, rescuing six survivors, but in bad weather the next morning clashed with escorting cruiser HMS *Trinidad* and destroyers HMS *Fury* and *Eclipse*. In a running battle, Z26 was severely damaged and later sunk, taking 243 crew to the bottom while 88 men, including Pönitz and captain Korvettenkapitän von Berger, were rescued. U376 later found eight more ships. In exchange for five of PQ13's 19 merchants being sunk (two by the Luftwaffe, one by destroyer and two by U-boats), Z26, U655 and U585 were sunk, the latter damaged by depth charges and then striking a German mine that had broken loose from its anchor, going down with all hands. It was a ruinous rate of exchange.

Suffering regular Soviet air bombardment, the small port and limited facilities of Kirkenes were clearly insufficient to accommodate an ever-increasing U-boat presence. A prime logistical problem facing U-boats in Kirkenes was the lack of immediate repair facilities. Although depot ships were able to provide a certain amount of rudimentary mechanical support, major repairs such as the kind of propeller damage drifting ice could inflict required a journey south to Trondheim and its extensive shipyard.

Instead, SKL planned for 20 U-boats to be committed to cover Norway: eight in the Iceland–Faeroes–Scotland area, six within the Arctic, two in Narvik, two in Trondheim and two in Bergen. Those on Arctic Sea operations would be directed by MGK Nord, those with stationary assignments by Commanding Admiral, Norway and those near the Faeroes remaining under B.d.U. control. Under pressure to supply these additional U-boats, Dönitz recommended the use of new boats nearing completion in Kiel and Wilhelmshaven.

Tirpitz; the largest battleship built by any European navy, pictured after arrival in Altafjord and before anti-torpedo nets were strung. (Author Collection)

The Kriegsmarine had already designated Kristiansand, Bergen, Trondheim, Tromsø and Kirkenes as suitable U-boat bases, and ordered each port occupied by two operational U-boats by the middle of February. Shortly thereafter, Narvik was added and, in January 1943, Hammerfest. Immediate results were dismal; the U-boats' combined achievement being the sinking of steam trawler *RT-19 'Komintern'* (1,180 tons) and three patrol boats.

In Narvik, relatively makeshift facilities were soon capable of complex repairs. However, the primary Norwegian U-boat base remained Trondheim, where construction of a bunker had already begun during summer 1941. The need for extensive dry-docking capability outside of Germany had become obvious, and the Dora I complex offered three dry docks and two wet pens, capable of holding seven boats at any one time. Dora II was planned but never reached completion. The logistics involved in building Dora I meant that it was not operational until July 1943. During November 1941, work had also begun on another shelter in Bergen – Bruno – containing six pens, half of them dry docks, finally being made operational in July 1944.

The crenulated Norwegian coastline was difficult for the security forces to patrol as they attempted to counter covert agent and commando landings. On 31 March 1943, a Räumboot intercepted Norwegian cutter *Brattholm* near Rebbenes in Karlsøy carrying a 12-man sabotage troop. The small Norwegian craft had escaped to Iceland during November 1940, and was later requisitioned by Norwegian authorities for service with the 'Shetland Bus', a clandestine ferry organization formed by SOE (the Special Operations Executive) for shuttling spies and equipment between Norwegian resistance groups. Attempting to escape, the cutter was hit by gunfire which killed one man and wounded two others, who later died in hospital. Scuttling their small craft, eight Norwegians were taken prisoner and subsequently interrogated, tortured and shot by the Gestapo, only one man successfully escaping to Sweden.

In March, the Arctic U-boats finally received their own dedicated command. Veteran skipper and former commander of Brest's 9th U-boat Flotilla, Kapitänleutnant Jürgen Oesten, began serving as U-boat Staff Officer to Admiral Nordmeer in Kirkenes. He remained at the post until January 1943, when F.d.U. Norway was finally established. To the south, handling the same duties for MGK Nord, veteran skipper and erstwhile commander of La Rochelle's 3rd U-boat Flotilla, Herbert Schultze, was assigned as U-boat Staff Officer. Furthermore, during May, the first Arctic Ocean flotilla was created, under the command of Hans Cohausz. Previously, Arctic boats had remained administratively

(Left to right) Vizeadmiral Hubert Schmundt (Admiral Nordmeer), Kapitänleutnant Jürgen Oesten (Unterseeboots-Asto – U-boat Staff Officer – on Schmundt's staff) and Kapitänleutnant Reinhard Reche, commander of U255, aboard the *Tanga* after the successful operation against PQ17. (Author Collection)

the same strength as flotillas in Germany and France, but with the creation of the 11th U-boat Flotilla, logistical matters transferred to Bergen, Cohausz no stranger to the requirements of a combat flotilla, having previously commanded Brest's 1st U-boat Flotilla.

Both PQ15 and QP11 were detected and attacked by U-boats and Luftwaffe bombers. Cruiser HMS *Edinburgh* of QP11's escort was damaged by two torpedoes from U456 and then attacked by three of Hinrichs's destroyers – *Z7 'Hermann Schoemann'*, Z24 and Z25. In fighting off Bear Island, *Edinburgh*'s escorting destroyers forced away two enemy destroyers while taking severe damage, and Z7 was sunk by gunfire from *Edinburgh*. The cruiser was then hit by a destroyer torpedo, abandoned and scuttled.

Germany's summer offensive opened on the southern Russian steppes in late June, and with Soviet forces in chaotic retreat, Stalin demanded greater supply from the Western Allies. PQ17 was assembled with 35 merchant ships under Royal Navy escort, and as it departed Iceland's mid-point stop, Oesten ordered four wolf pack *Eisteufel* boats to locate and shadow while six others formed a patrol line across its expected path. Outbound QP13 was located but ignored in favour of the incoming laden merchants. U255 shadowed PQ17 and others were given freedom to attack but were thwarted by escorts and poor marksmanship.

The Kriegsmarine, determined to throw everything at PQ17, organized Operation *Rösselsprung*, activating *Tirpitz* and *Admiral Hipper*, which departed Trondheim to move north in preparation. Their movement was detected by Allied intelligence as they joined *Admiral Scheer* awaiting orders to sail against PQ17. On 4 July, the convoy suffered its first casualties to Luftwaffe attack. American freighter *Christopher Newport* was damaged and abandoned, then located by Karl Brandenburg's U457 and sunk with a single torpedo. Liberty ship *William Hooper* was similarly damaged and abandoned, subsequently being sunk by Hilmar Siemon's U334. The number of vessels damaged by Luftwaffe torpedoes but later sunk by a U-boat was quite high as airborne torpedoes and their warheads were smaller, only 45cm in diameter compared to the 53.34cm of U-boat torpedoes.

While the Kriegsmarine refused to order the heavy ships of *Rösselsprung* into action until the whereabouts of enemy carriers could be ascertained, Oesten's U-boats were thrown against PQ17. In Altafjord, Admiral Otto Schniewind aboard *Tirpitz* seethed at his inability to put to sea and join battle until 1500hrs on 5 July, when he was finally granted permission to sail. *Tirpitz* and *Admiral Hipper*, with destroyers *Friedrich Ihn*, *Hans Lody*, *Karl Galster* and *Theodor Riedel*, along with torpedo boats T7 and T15, then departed for Altafjord, where, before attacking PQ17, they would join the battle group from Narvik under the command of Vizeadmiral Oskar Kummetz that comprised heavy cruisers *Lützow* and *Admiral Scheer* escorted by destroyers Z24, Z27, Z28, Z29 and Z30. During the outward voyage, destroyers *Hans Lody*, *Karl Galster* and

Theodor Riedel all grounded on rocks and were forced to return to port, as was *Lützow* in Narvik.

Sighted by British Catalina flying boats and submarines, messages intercepted by B-Dienst (the German radio-listening service) caused consternation in Berlin. Following an unsuccessful Soviet submarine attack on *Tirpitz*, and after only six hours at sea, Raeder ordered the ships recalled. Unbeknown to them, news in Britain that *Tirpitz* had sailed had caused virtual panic within the Admiralty. A series of escalating messages, withdrawing the escorts, culminated in tragedy at 2136hrs when PQ17 was ordered to scatter.

Despite the convoy having successfully driven off repeated air attacks, albeit at the loss of four merchants, they were now ordered to disperse and lose the collective defence at the heart of the convoying principle. To make matters worse, the weather had cleared. The result was devastating. As the first PQ17 survivor made landfall in Archangelsk on 13 July, thick fog at the entrance to the White Sea brought operations against PQ17 to an end. Oesten directed U-boats to find whatever scattered merchants remained, five boats combing the area and sinking the final U-boat casualty from PQ17 that day, the 7,168-ton *Paulus Potter*.

Of the 34 ships that had departed Iceland, 24 had been sunk: 16 by U-boats and the remainder by the Luftwaffe. Statistically, in terms of tonnage sunk, it was the most successful U-boat convoy attack of the war. Five Luftwaffe aircraft had been lost, while the U-boats suffered no casualties. Soviet authorities accused the Royal Navy of cowardice and dishonesty about the number of ships lost, while in Washington Admiral King was enraged at the destruction of 14 American ships and refused to cooperate with the Royal Navy any further within the region, moving his forces to the Pacific.

Officers and crew on deck of *Tirpitz*, moored in Norway. In the background are camouflaged floats that were used to help hide the ship from Allied reconnaissance. (Naval History and Heritage Command)

The next inbound convoy, PQ18, was postponed until September as the Royal Navy focussed on Mediterranean operations. The convoy was sighted on 8 September by long-range aerial reconnaissance, whereupon Operation *Doppelschlag* began, involving *Admiral Scheer*, *Admiral Hipper*, light cruiser *Köln* and six destroyers. Sailing north to Altafjord, they awaited clearance to attack. They planned to form two battle groups, the first drawing away any major escorting forces, while the second engaged the convoy. Aboard *Scheer*, Vizeadmiral Kummetz pressed for permission to sail, until Raeder deemed that their freedom of action was so compromised by Hitler's 'no unnecessary risks' stance that he cancelled the operation, leaving PQ18 to U-boats and aircraft.

Though three PQ18 ships would later be sunk by U-boats and another ten by the Luftwaffe, the price was heavy: three U-boats and 49 aircraft were destroyed. Of the Luftwaffe's entire complement of trained torpedo bomber crews, 42 per cent of them had been lost in action against PQ18; the Luftwaffe was never again able to mount such strong attacks on Russian convoys. Nonetheless, the severe losses accrued by both PQ17 and PQ18, coupled with Allied naval demands of Operation *Torch*, led to the suspension of the Arctic convoys until December 1942.

On 23 July, common sense prevailed and SKL authorized the return of 6th S-Flotilla to the west, *Adolf Lüderitz* remaining in Norway for its radio capabilities. An expected operation involving the S-boats to land Wehrmacht troops on the Rybachy Peninsula and kick-start the land attack against Murmansk had been repeatedly postponed – gradually edging towards final cancellation in 1944 – and with no useful role left, the flotilla was transferred.

Admiral Scheer sailed on 16 August from Narvik on Operation *Wunderland*, bound for the Kara Sea. Intelligence indicated that many Soviet vessels sheltered from pack ice in this region, and *Scheer*'s mission was to attack and destroy these ships and bombard Soviet ports within the region. Accompanying the cruiser during the first leg of its voyage were three destroyers and two U-boats, while two more despatched to the seas off Novaya Zemlya, partially to divert enemy attention from the cruiser.

On 24 August, after a personal meeting between *Scheer*'s captain, Kapitän zur See Wilhelm Meendsen-Bohlken, and U601's Kapitänleutnant Peter Grau to exchange weather and ice information, U601 torpedoed 2,332-ton Soviet freighter *Kujbyshev* north-west of Port Dikson. A 50-ton harbour tug being towed by the steamer *Medvezhonok* was also sunk after the boat surfaced and hit it with 20 rounds from the 88mm deck gun. Meanwhile, *Scheer* experienced little success, sinking a Soviet icebreaker but failing to find further targets. The cruiser bombarded Soviet military installations at Port Dikson, but despite badly damaging two ships and wrecking several buildings, the impact of the attack was transitory and ultimately *Wunderland* achieved little. *Scheer* returned to Kirkenes and then Narvik.

Admiral Hipper returned to the region in September. Following the loss of minelayer *Ulm*, *Hipper* was pressed into minelaying service for Operation *Zarin* to sow a field of 96 mines off the islands of Novaya Zemlya. Commanded by Vizeadmiral Oskar Kummetz, Kapitän zur See Wilhelm Meisel's *Hipper* sailed under escort by Z23, Z28, Z29 and Z30 and successfully laid its minefield on the north-west coast of Novaya Zemlya.

With the Soviet Union still clamouring for Allied supplies, the Arctic convoys were resumed in what the Royal Navy hoped would be the advantageous environment of the Arctic winter night, now codenamed 'JW' for outbound and 'RA' for those headed back to the United Kingdom. JW51A departed Loch Ewe on 15 December, all 15 merchants arriving at the Kola Inlet on Christmas Day after an unopposed and idyllic sailing. On 22 December,

Survivors of Soviet ice breaker *Aleksandr Sibiryakov* are rescued by *Admiral Scheer*'s launch after the cruiser sank it with gunfire on 25 August 1942 during Operation *Wunderland*. (Naval History and Heritage Command)

14 merchant ships of JW51B departed Scotland and were detected by Luftwaffe aircraft on Christmas Eve in stormy weather. U-boats subsequently shadowed as heavy ships were readied once again to sail.

Operation *Regenbogen* was now launched by cruisers *Lützow* and *Admiral Hipper* and six destroyers, the debacle that followed sealing the fates of both the surface fleet and Erich Raeder. After repeated messages reminding him of Hitler's 'no unnecessary risks' directive, the cruisers perfectly performed the same plan of attack as *Doppelschlag* but were unwilling to engage as British cruisers neared, being driven off by Royal Navy destroyers that damaged *Admiral Hipper* and sank destroyer *Friederich Eckoldt*. In turn destroyer HMS *Achates* and minesweeper HMS *Bramble* were sunk, but the convoy suffered no damage.

When Hitler learned of the failure, he exploded in a fit of apoplectic rage. Sporadic communications throughout the unfolding battle had already led him to believe that the Kriegsmarine was in the process of eliminating the convoy. With the military situation dire in all land theatres, Hitler had clung to his premature conclusions that at last promised a glimmer of good news. The consequences of his disappointment were far reaching, as Hitler ranted uncontrollably and demanded Germany's surface fleet be scrapped and the guns used ashore. Within days, Grossadmiral Raeder had become aware that whatever influence he once had with the German dictator was at an end and he resigned. His vacant position of Oberbefehlshaber der Kriegsmarine was taken by Karl Dönitz on 31 January 1943.

1943

Dönitz's appointment did not mark the dramatic turning point in Kriegsmarine policy that many had expected. While he obviously favoured U-boat power over surface forces, it was he who convinced Hitler to cancel his decision to scrap Germany's fleet. Dönitz realized that there was no appreciable gain in manpower or resources from the loss of the big ships and that their very existence still posed a threat to the Allies. To Hitler's annoyance, Dönitz withdrew his support for the idea and argued the proposal be cancelled, instead advocating the formation of a battle squadron comprising *Tirpitz*, *Scharnhorst* and *Lützow* be gathered in Norway to defend the country from potential invasion and assist fighting on the Eastern Front by intercepting Arctic convoys. Hitler resentfully relented.

OPERATION *WUNDERLAND*, AUGUST 1942

On 16 August (**1**) *Admiral Scheer* leaves Narvik with escorting destroyers *Richard Beitzen, Erich Steinbrinck* and *Friedrich Eckoldt*. They head south to deceive enemy reconnaissance. The destroyers soon detach to head for Tromsø (**2**). On 17 August U209 attacks a NKVD convoy of four vessels (**3**) and sinks them with gunfire. 305 men are killed and 23 survivors are later rescued by a Soviet ship. On the 19th *Admiral Scheer* makes rendezvous (**4**) with U601 early morning to receive ice information, followed the next day with U251 (**5**) to receive local information. The cruiser is informed that its smoke is visible for 20 miles. The same day U456 attacks (**6**) Soviet icebreaker *SKR-18/Fyodor Litke* off Whale Bay, but torpedoes miss. The vessel is depth-charged by escorts but escapes by diving under the ice.

On 23 August, *Scheer*'s Arado aircraft sights (**7**) convoy traffic which is later lost in fog. The Arado is lost in a landing accident. Thick fog forces *Admiral Scheer* to temporarily drop anchor amidst heavy ice. On 24 August U601 sinks (**8**) Soviet merchant ship *Kuybyshev* and tug *Medvezhonok* west of Port Dikson. On 25 August, U255 destroys a Soviet wireless station on Cape Zhelaniya with gunfire (**9**), while (**10**) *Admiral Scheer* sinks Soviet icebreaker *Aleksandr Sibiryakov* carrying fuel, equipment, food, and a change of polar explorers from Port Dikson to Severnaya Zemlya.

On 28 August MGK Nord signals (**11**) orders for *Scheer* to begin its return journey at noon on 29 August. The ship breaks wireless silence to request a delay, allowing a sweep to be made towards Spitzbergen but is denied. The same day U209 bombards (**12**) the wireless station and octagonal lighthouse at Khodovarikha, while U589 lays mines (**13**) at the west end of the Matochkin Strait. Soviet naval trawler *SKR-23 Musson* is subsequently sunk by one of these mines on 11 October with the loss of 25 crew.

On 29 August (**14**) B-Dienst (German radio listening service) records a large volume of wireless transmissions from Port Dikson to merchant shipping following *Scheer*'s attack on *Aleksandr Sibiryakov*. Kommodore Wilhelm Meendsen-Bohlken, *Scheer*'s captain, deduces the port as essential for Soviet Arctic convoys and decides to attack it. Port Dikson is shelled, guard ship *Deznev* hit and damaged, six crew are killed. Ultimately, damage is relatively superficial and has no real impact on convoy traffic. *Deznev* returns to service three days later.

On 29 August *Admiral Scheer* makes rendezvous (**15**) with escorting destroyers *Friedrich Eckoldt, Erich Steinbrinck* and *Richard Beitzen*, reaching Kirkenes the following day.

On 18 January, Kapitän zur See Rudolf Peters took charge of the newly created post of F.d.U. Norwegen from the former state yacht *Grille* in Narvik harbour. Narvik remained a centre point for Arctic operations, and three 28cm cannons had been installed in heavy defensive batteries alongside myriad bunkers of the most northerly portion of the Atlantic Wall and a newly established naval hospital staffed with seven full-time doctors. For the 11th U-boat Flotilla, two Type VIIF transport U-boats with extended hulls – U1060 and U1061 – were used for frequent torpedo resupply trips from Germany.

During February, Boehm's office was redesignated Marineoberkommando Norwegen, and Boehm departed during the following month, returning to Germany two months before retiring from active service. In his place as Oberbefehlshaber der MOK Norwegen came Admiral Otto Ciliax.

Sporadic successes against Arctic convoys failed to justify the number of U-boats deployed; RA53, scattered by atrocious weather, losing the most ships with three American freighters sunk. Not until March did Operation *Paderborn* see deployment of *Scharnhorst* to the Arctic, the ship arriving with destroyer escort on 9 March in Bogen Bay and anchoring near *Lützow*, in line with Dönitz's decision to form his Norwegian battle group. *Nürnberg* was also present in northern Norway until April 1943, when it returned to Germany, never to leave the Baltic again.

Despite Hitler's reluctance, Dönitz had even attained a certain measure of autonomy and tactical freedom for the *Scharnhorst* and removal of Hitler's severe restrictions. British intelligence had noted the ship's arrival and – fearing a more aggressive stance from Dönitz – advised against further Arctic convoys as the lengthy days of summer approached. The Admiralty agreed and the JW convoys were suspended during March.

Recurrent diesel problems forced *Lützow* to return to Germany for repairs, leaving *Scharnhorst* and *Tirpitz* as the only major ships present in Norwegian waters. Germany's critical fuel shortages kept its surface forces largely idle in Norwegian waters. Destroyers – now reinforced by elements of 4th Destroyer Flotilla – averaged just two days at sea per month, generally escorting minelayers. Training standards suffered and Operation *Zitronella* was mounted as much to restore flagging morale as any genuine military necessity. On 6 September, under the command of Admiral Kummetz, *Tirpitz*, *Scharnhorst* and nine destroyers from all three flotillas sailed from Altafjord for Spitzbergen, where 600 men of the 349th Grenadier Regiment would be landed under covering fire. Their objective was the destruction of a small Norwegian army base, shore installations and meteorological stations. It was the last major Kriegsmarine task force to sail during World War II.

The battleships shelled targets ashore and covered the landing parties that successfully destroyed Norwegian installations and took 31 prisoners, with six Norwegians killed. The Germans suffered 16 wounded sailors, one of whom later died, and another destroyer crewman was court-martialled and sentenced to death for cowardice. He was executed on *Scharnhorst*'s quarterdeck. By late afternoon on 9 September, the squadron was back in Altafjord, and within a month the Allies had re-established their Spitzbergen bases.

A Marinefahrprähme unloading equipment in Rypefjord near Hammerfest during the spring of 1943. Marinefahrprähme provided excellent transport capability for short-haul voyages and could be readily converted to patrol vessels and artillery carriers (Artilleriefahrprähme). (Finnmark Fylkesbibliotek)

In Berlin, SKL debated whether to return *Tirpitz* to Germany for refit or for the mighty warship to undergo a longer refitting period in less well-equipped Norwegian harbours. However, on 22 September, *Tirpitz*, lying in Kåfjord, was disabled by charges laid beneath the ship using newly developed British X-Craft midget submarines in Operation *Source*. Though five of the deployed X-Craft were destroyed, *Tirpitz* suffered significant damage requiring extensive repairs. Danzig and Kiel shipyards were already at capacity and ports further west too vulnerable to air attack, so *Tirpitz* was ordered to be repaired in situ. After exceptional engineering work from technicians aboard the repair ship *Neumark*, it was returned to fighting strength by April 1944.

While *Tirpitz* remained out of service, *Scharnhorst* was the sole serviceable major ship. On 19 December, to vindicate his decision to maintain this battle group, Dönitz announced to Hitler that *Scharnhorst* and destroyers would be used against the next Arctic convoy 'if a successful operation seems assured'. Disastrously, Dönitz decided that an attack on inbound convoy JW55B, sighted sporadically by aircraft and U-boats, presented just such an opportunity. Invoking the spectre of supporting the Eastern Front, the attack was codenamed Operation *Ostfront*.

Vizeadmiral Kummetz had departed for extended sick leave in Germany and been replaced as battle group commander by destroyer leader Konteradmiral Erich Bey, a man of great experience, but all of which was aboard destroyers. He had never served aboard either a cruiser or battleship, and had no experience

SCHARNHORST, TIRPITZ AND *LÜTZOW* ENTER ALTAFJORD, OPERATION *SILESIA*, 23 MARCH 1943

On 24 March 1943, the SKL War Diary recorded: *'The transfer to Alta of the formation of Commanding Admiral, Task Force has been carried out according to plan (Operation Silesia).' Scharnhorst, Tirpitz* and *Lützow* were to use Altafjord as their base of operations, with Admiral Oskar Kummetz as the force commander aboard *Tirpitz*.

Six escorting destroyers of the 6th Destroyer Flotilla accompanied the three large ships into the Norwegian fjord, Kapitän zur See Alfred Schulze-Hinrichs aboard flotilla lead ship *Z5 'Paul Jacobi'*.

Nürnberg was intended to join the group, but returned to Germany instead. Meanwhile, recurrent diesel problems forced *Lützow* to return to Germany for repairs, leaving *Scharnhorst* and *Tirpitz* as the only major ships present in Norwegian waters, They remained inactive until September 1943 and the attack on Spitzbergen.

in the use of large-calibre guns. To compound his problems, the staff of the battle group had been thinned of experienced officers as SKL expected the ships to see little action. Even Kapitän zur See Fritz Hintze, *Scharnhorst* captain and previously navigation officer aboard *Admiral Hipper*, had only arrived in October after a year within the torpedo research centre. Bey gathered the most experienced officers from *Tirpitz* and boarded *Scharnhorst*, which sailed as ordered on Christmas Day, escorted by five destroyers of 4th Flotilla. Weather conditions were deteriorating rapidly and Bey knew that the destroyers would soon be unable to effectively operate; unexpectedly breaking radio silence to report a destroyer was likely to be gravely impaired. Dönitz's reply was unequivocal that the convoy must be attacked, and that he remained 'confident of [Bey's] offensive spirit'. Though the usual caveat of permission to disengage if encountering heavy forces was included, the instructions were clear and *Scharnhorst* sailed onward.

The forward triple 28cm SK C/34 gun turrets aboard *Scharnhorst*, photographed here in Kiel. (Naval History and Heritage Command)

Commander-in-chief of the Royal Navy Home Fleet, Admiral Sir Bruce Fraser, had hoped that JW55B would draw out *Scharnhorst*. After excellent ULTRA intelligence revealed the battleship at sea, Fraser planned to trap Bey between a strong force centred on battleship HMS *Duke of York* and Vice-Admiral Robert Burnett's cruiser screen for JW55B that remained near the convoy.

During early morning on 26 December, in worsening weather, Bey was frustrated in his attempts to find the convoy, detaching the destroyers who were struggling in the heavy seas in order to widen the search. They were never to rejoin *Scharnhorst*, which continued alone. At 0900hrs, HMS *Belfast* detected *Scharnhorst* on its radar and Burnett's cruisers engaged within half an hour. The British possessed radar-controlled gunnery and were using flashless powder, making them almost impossible to detect. A British shell destroyed *Scharnhorst*'s *Seetakt* radar, forcing Bey to fight blind in driving snow squalls as he broke away to attempt to find JW55B. A second clash several hours later with Burnett's cruisers saw HMS *Norfolk* hit and its radar disabled, Bey breaking away once again but heading straight for *Duke of York*, which soon acquired radar contact. As *Belfast* fired star shells, *Duke of York* opened fire at considerable distance, disabling *Scharnhorst*'s forward turrets and destroying the hangar. A hit in the boiler room reduced its speed. Destroyers then fired torpedoes, hitting *Scharnhorst* and further reducing its speed. As *Duke of York* closed again, HMS *Belfast* and *Jamaica* added torpedoes to the attack, and at 1945hrs *Scharnhorst* sank.

Bey and Hintze were among the last to abandon ship, Hintze giving his lifejacket to a junior seaman who had mislaid his. Both were later seen in the water; neither survived. Only 36 survivors were rescued, with more than 1,900 men perishing. *Tirpitz*, once again, remained the solitary surface threat in the north of Norway.

1944

Tirpitz returned to service during April after repairs, whereupon several carrier operations were mounted by the Fleet Air Arm against the battleship in its Kåfjord anchorage. Operation *Tungsten* took place on 3 April, when 21 Fairey Barracudas achieved complete surprise and attacked with mixed-weight armour piercing, semi-armour piercing and anti-submarine bombs, the latter capable of causing concussion damage below the waterline. In total, 14 direct hits were scored despite low cloud, a smokescreen and the fjord's confined airspace. While *Tirpitz*'s main armour was not penetrated, significant damage was caused, with two 15cm gun turrets destroyed, the starboard turbine disabled, fires breaking out and 2,000 tons of water flooding through the splinter-damaged hull side. All four of the ship's Arado Ar 196A-5 reconnaissance aircraft were destroyed, killing one aircraft crewmember, while at least 121 of *Tirpitz*'s crew were killed, with around 300 others wounded. Four British aircraft were lost and nine men killed, but *Tirpitz* was incapacitated for three months.

Repairs were made once again, but the Fleet Air Arm continued the assault with repeated attacks in July and August. Minor damage was inflicted by each attack, but German observer posts established in the outer fjord gave a minimum 14-minute warning of each attack, allowing watertight doors to be closed and prearranged 'box-fire' anti-aircraft barrages prepared. Thick smokescreens were generally well established by the time of the British arrival, and both heavy anti-aircraft fire and low cloud ceiling reduced the effectiveness of each attack. Several bombs that did strike the ship were also found to be duds.

In Narvik, at the beginning of May, Rudolf Peters departed as F.d.U. Norwegen, replaced by veteran U-boat officer Korvettenkapitän Reinhard 'Teddy' Suhren. Initially, Suhren was dismayed that Narvik U-boats were forced to make a journey of nearly 2,000km to Trondheim or Bergen for maintenance, while repair ships stationed in Narvik were underutilized, despite their engineering crews of civilian workers and military personnel being capable of extremely high working standards. The northbound railway line ended at Trondheim, making it impossible to supply enough materiel to Narvik, and Suhren's appeals to Admiral Nordmeer, Konteradmiral Otto Klüber,

Crewmen camouflaging *Tirpitz* as it lay in Fættenfjord after arrival in Norway, January 1942. (Naval History and Heritage Command)

for dedicated supply shipping fell on deaf ears. Undeterred, Suhren appealed directly to Reichskommissar Terboven, who swiftly secured him a small coastal steamer, raising some ire from Klüber and his staff.

By September 1944, the Kriegsmarine was virtually a spent force, much of the months that followed providing nothing but a tragic postscript to a war extended beyond Germany's capabilities. In the west, the French U-boat bases had either been captured, abandoned or besieged and were no longer viable operational ports. The U-boats themselves were virtually obsolete, as Allied technology had outpaced German developments on the front line. Suhren's position of F.d.U. Norwegen had become F.d.U. Nordmeer during August following the arrival of F.d.U. West, relocating from France to Bergen. The surviving western boats were transferred to Norway or Germany, F.d.U. West, responsible for logistics, supporting those that continued the fight outside of Arctic waters.

Another wasteful deployment of S-boats to Norway happened during October. MOK Norwegen had continually request S-boats to protect *Tirpitz* and for use in coastal defence. Denied by SKL, an executive decision made at Führer headquarters could not be ignored and the 4th S-Flotilla was despatched to northern Norway. Severe weather resulted in S203 colliding with an R-boat near Lindesnes, the boat being abandoned and scuttled, and damage to four other S-boats sustained while rescuing the crew.

Nonetheless, MOK Norwegen pressed for a second flotilla to be sent north for ASW work. The 1st S-Training Flotilla was earmarked for transfer. However, rather than the depleted 4th S-Flotilla continuing its journey north, it was transferred to the jurisdiction of Admiral Westküste to satisfy the ASW requirements, while the training boats were assigned to the polar seas. However, Germany's Ardennes offensive and demand for total S-boat combat commitment in the west saw 4th S-Flotilla returned to The Netherlands. Meanwhile, 1st S-Training Flotilla arrived in southern Norway, remaining there as convoy escorts until the war's end. It was an exercise in futile waste that resulted in the destruction of a single ship on 29 March 1945, when S13 accidentally fired a torpedo that hit and sank 543-ton Norwegian passenger ship *Kommandøren* in Bergen harbour.

Meanwhile, in Britain, the task of destroying *Tirpitz* had been passed to RAF Bomber Command. Lancaster bombers of Nos 9 and 617 Squadrons were earmarked for operations, using a combination of 12,000lb 'Tallboy' bombs and 'Johnny Walker' Diving

Admiral von Schrader distributes Iron Crosses to crew men of U703 at Bergen, Norway, following the battle against convoy PQ17. On the far left is the U-boat's captain, Kapitänleutnant Heinz Bielfeld. After leaving U702, he was killed in action as commander of U1222 in the Bay of Biscay on 11 July 1944. U702 was listed as missing with all hands on 16 September 1944. (Naval History and Heritage Command)

Mines. Due to the sheer distance and heavy payloads involved, the 38 RAF bombers assigned were instructed to stage through Yagodnik airfield in the Soviet Union near Arkhangelsk, flying directly there from the United Kingdom, from where accurate weather forecasts could be made before the actual raid.

Operation *Paravane* took place on 15 September, when 27 armed Lancasters and another from the Film Unit (463 Squadron) took off for Kåfjord, being detected by German radar ten minutes before reaching *Tirpitz*. A thick defensive smokescreen obscured most of the target and ferocious anti-aircraft fire arced skywards, including shells fired from *Tirpitz*'s main guns. Out of 21 Tallboys dropped, only one caused any damage, although it was enough to bring about the end of *Tirpitz* as a maritime threat. The bomb hit the upper bow deck to starboard, passing out of the hull through the flare of the forecastle and detonating in the water below keel level. The blast destroyed a significant portion of the forecastle, flooding the ship's forepart. Though *Tirpitz*'s machinery remained intact, structural damage could not be repaired without dry dock and thus *Tirpitz* could no longer take to the open sea. The great ship was no longer a threat to Arctic convoys and had therefore ceased to be the Germans' northern 'fleet in being'.

Tirpitz now functioned solely as a floating battery, as during September German forces had begun to withdraw from Finnmark following Finland's armistice with the Soviet Union. Among the terms dictated by Stalin's government was the expulsion of all German troops from Finland, thus beginning the 'Lapland War'. Though the loss of the Petsamo mines dealt a significant blow to the German war economy, the Wehrmacht could not hold the existing front line against Soviet and Finnish troops, and the Germans mounted a scorched earth retreat. Anything deemed potentially useful to the Red Army was destroyed, from livestock to houses and telegraph poles. Soviet troops captured Petsamo after German troops had sabotaged the mines on 15 October, and Kirkenes was demolished and abandoned by the Germans ten days later.

Relaxing in Kirkenes harbour. (Naval History and Heritage Command)

A new defensive line was established at Lyngenfjord, where a range of mountains created a natural barrier just east of Tromsø and hundreds of fortified bunkers were hurriedly constructed by forced labour. Hammerfest, the most northerly remaining U-boat port, was abandoned in October, the U-boat base moving to Kilbotn, south of Harstad, and the town burnt to the ground as its Norwegian inhabitants were forcibly moved south.

Since the destruction of *Scharnhorst*, 4th Destroyer Flotilla had remained largely inactive in company with *Tirpitz*, bolstering its anti-aircraft defences. During October, the destroyers had added fire support to the German troops retreating from Finnmark, also covering maritime evacuations during this period. The evacuations were considerably eased by the addition of 9th Landing Flotilla to Seekommandant Narvik's command and 6th L-Flotilla to Seekommandant Hammerfest in June, then 5th L-Flotilla to Seekommandant Kirkenes and 7th L-Flotilla to Seekommandant Tromsø in July, followed by 8th L-Flotilla being moved to Tromsø in August. The Marinefahrprähme of the Landing Flotillas provided relatively inexpensive patrol craft while also vastly improving local maritime transport capabilities. On 11 November, SKL recorded:

> *'Staff Admiral Polar Coast has moved to Finfjordbotn; the command staff initially remaining mobile between front-line locations with bases in Alta, Tromsø, and Finfjordbotn. After the occupation of the Lyngen position, Finfjordbotn will also become the base for the command staff.*
>
> *Between 11 and 31 October, 509 east–west journeys were made across the Lyngenfjord, carrying 9,973 men, 209 horses, 1,640 trucks, 779 cars and motorcycles, 12 tanks, 97 horse-drawn vehicles, 20 guns, and 1,394 tons of Wehrmacht equipment. [In the same period] 492 west–east journeys were made across the Lyngenfjord, carrying 3,492 men, 732 trucks, 324 cars, and others. 44 ships convoy[ed] successfully to the north and 26 to the south.'*

Tirpitz was deemed vulnerably close to the front line, and during October a different anchorage was found next to the southern shore of Håkøya island. There, it was felt that the full range of *Tirpitz*'s artillery could be utilized for bombardment in support of nearby ground forces, while additional anti-aircraft guns and smoke protection due for installation would also benefit the nearby port of Tromsø. However, where natural fjord contours of previous anchorages had helped shelter *Tirpitz* from air attack, Håkøya and the nearby land masses were flat and offered little protection. Nevertheless, *Tirpitz* moved to Sandessundet on 15 October, under the codename Operation *Comet*, after the damaged bow had been strengthened to a degree that would allow a maximum speed of 8 knots. Luftflotte 5 aircraft reconnoitred the route to be taken, and with 4th Destroyer Flotilla on alert in Tverrfjord south of Silda, the battleship departed in company with heavy floating anti-aircraft artillery batteries *Nymphe* and *Thetis* and under strong escort. The anti-aircraft and smoke defences at Kåfjord were to be dismantled and rebuilt at the new anchorage, *Tirpitz* retaining all its own anti-aircraft artillery aboard.

Crew of the flak ship *Nymphe* on parade. The larger stern searchlight is obvious, with only one of the two smaller forward searchlights visible in this view. (Naval History and Heritage Command)

Tirpitz reached its new anchorage at 1500hrs on 16 October, whereupon approximately 600 men, the majority of them engine room personnel, were removed, leaving about 1,700 crew members still aboard as torpedo nets were strung around the ship.

Tirpitz's new location was reported by Norwegian resistance and a second raid by Nos 9 and 617 Squadron Lancasters was mounted on 29 October. Thirty-nine Tallboy-armed Lancasters from the two squadrons, again accompanied by a photo-reconnaisance Lancaster of 463 Squadron, launched Operation *Obviate*, ironically foiled by cloud cover over *Tirpitz*, whose artificial smoke generators were not yet operational. Not a single bomb hit the concealed battleship, though a near miss off the port quarter damaged the port shaft and rudder and caused some flooding, injuring three men.

On *Tirpitz*, the generally low state of morale was raised somewhat as the crew believed their own anti-aircraft fire had prevented British success. Undeterred by this failure, the RAF mounted an identical operation, *Catechism*, on 12 November. The bombers arrived over *Tirpitz* at 0941hrs, and though heavy anti-aircraft fire greeted them, there were no functioning smokescreen generators and visibility was perfect. Eight minutes later, the last bomb had fallen, two direct hits impacting the ship and one landing alongside.

One Tallboy landed to the port of Bruno turret and did not explode, while the second struck amidships to port and detonated over the boiler room, causing severe damage and extensive flooding which produced a strong list. A third may have hit the armoured deck near Caesar turret, possibly detonating a magazine as the entire turret was blown clear of the ship. *Tirpitz*'s captain, Kapitän zur See Robert Weber, ordered the lower ship evacuated as the list to port reached nearly 40°. Five minutes later, at 0950hrs, as the list worsened, he ordered the ship abandoned, *Tirpitz* finally rolling over and capsizing within the next two minutes. Of the crew, 596 swam to shore or were picked up, while a further 87 were later cut free from the upturned hull. Emergency lighting within the capsized ship only lasted for six hours, any remaining time was spent in darkness, with rising cold water and dwindling oxygen. Such rescue efforts were suspended after 24 hours as available oxygen inside the hull was considered expended. The exact number of casualties remains unknown, estimates ranging between 940 and 1,204 men killed, including Kapitän zur See Weber. As the ship had begun to capsize, Weber had ordered all hands on deck, but he and the crew of the forward combat command post were trapped after the heavy armoured hatches could not be opened. Only one staff officer escaped.

RAF Coastal Command had transferred seven squadrons of anti-shipping aircraft from eastern England to northern Scotland during September and October 1944. Three were equipped with Mosquito fighter-bombers and stationed at RAF Banff, while

Kapitän zur See Robert Weber, final commander of the *Tirpitz*. Former First Officer aboard *Tirpitz* and Staff Officer from *Admiral Nordmeer*, 40-year-old Weber went down with his ship. (Author Collection)

Minenräumschiffe 26 sinking after attack by Soviet A-20 bombers on 27 October 1944 that caused enough damage for the captain to run the ship aground on the north-east side of Hopsfjord before it capsized. An R-boat of the 7th R-Flotilla is engaged in rescuing survivors. Thirty-seven men were killed. (Finnmark Fylkesbibliotek)

four operated Beaufighter heavy fighters from RAF Dallachy. The Banff Strike Wing swiftly made its presence felt against German convoys trailing along the Norwegian coast, forcing them to only sail at night and take shelter in deep fjords during daylight, where they were difficult to attack and frequently covered by anti-aircraft positions.

In southern Norway, German destroyers continued sporadic minelaying and escort duties under pressure from the Coastal Command strike wings and RAF minelaying. On 20 October, Z30 struck a mine while escorting freighters into Oslofjord. It was later towed to Oslo with severe damage, eight men having been killed and 16 badly injured. The destroyer was never repaired. By the year's end, only two destroyers remained serviceable as the remainder underwent repairs or refitting.

The 14th U-boat Flotilla had, in the meantime, been established in Narvik under the command of Knight's Cross holder Korvettenkapitän Helmut Möhlmann, former skipper of U571. The flotilla numbered only eight boats during its brief existence: U294, U295, U299, U318, U427, U716, U995 and U997. During December, they turned east along the Kola coast, hunting for Soviet targets. Russian submarines had been attempting to interfere with German convoys involved in the evacuation of Finland, and the 14th U-boat Flotilla sailed as many ASW vessels as commerce raiders.

1945

The destroyers of Kapitän zur See von Wangenheim's 4th Flotilla were ordered back to Germany during January, Z31, Z34 and Z38 sailing from Tromsø on 25 January. The temporarily disabled Z33 remained in Bogen Bay, Narvik, transmitting dummy messages to attempt to cover the remaining ships' departure. Nevertheless, ULTRA intelligence betrayed the move and the three were attacked by cruisers HMS *Diadem* and *Mauritius* north of Bergen in early morning darkness. The destroyers raced for the Norwegian coast, and despite hitting both cruisers with gunfire and causing some damage, Z31 was severely hit by shellfire before coastal artillery opened fire on the attackers and drove them away. Z31 was docked in Bergen for repairs, finally reaching Germany during March.

The last northern destroyer, Z33, left Narvik on 5 February. On the morning of 9 February, two New Zealand Beaufighters of 489 Squadron, patrolling the Norwegian coast, sighted scattered merchant shipping and Z33, accompanied by a minesweeper and two Vorpostenboote in Førde Fjord. ULTRA had already flagged the destroyer's movement, and the Dallachy Wing – under Admiralty operational control and instructed to prioritize warships over merchantmen – was ordered to attack.

As the aircraft approached, the German ships withdrew deeper into the narrow, well-defended fjord, anchoring close to the steep southern slopes near the village of Bjørkedal and covered by shore-based flak. Thirty-two Beaufighters, 12 P-51 Mustang escorts and two Warwick air-sea rescue aircraft passed over the anchorage and were met by intense anti-aircraft fire. The fjord's terrain restricted attack runs, and the arrival of 12 Fw 190s made the situation worse for the attackers. The Mustangs, initially caught by surprise, engaged, and the action became the largest aerial battle fought over Norway.

By the end, shipboard flak had shot down seven Beaufighters; Luftwaffe fighters claimed two more Beaufighters and a Mustang. Z33 was damaged, with four men killed. The Vorpostenboote were also hit – *V6808 'Rugier'* lost three men – and five Fw 190s were shot down. Nonetheless, the action of 9 February, later known as 'Black Friday', produced the heaviest losses suffered by any Coastal Command strike wing in a single operation. Z33 reached Trondheim on 11 February for repairs, sailing for Germany on 26 March and arriving at Swinemünde on 2 April. It saw no further combat and was decommissioned at Brunsbüttel in late April as the Kriegsmarine lacked fuel.

The sole naval threat from Norway came from U-boats. However, their effectiveness was minimal. From the entire 'JW' series of convoys, 159 merchant ships had reached the Soviet Union without loss. Of the returning 'RA' ships, only two had been sunk.

In desperation, during December 1944, *Molch* midget submarines of the Kleinkampfverbände (Small Battle Units) were deployed in Norway (415th K-Flotilla), held for coastal defence but seeing no action. However, in January 1945, an audacious plan was developed to use *Biber* one-man midget submarines from the 265th K-Flotilla, along with three boats of the 13th U-boat Flotilla, to attack Soviet battleship *Arkhangelsk* in Murmansk. Two *Bibers* each were to be carried atop the stern decks of U295, U716 and U739 to within striking range of the Soviet port, the operation – codenamed *Caesar* – planned for 5 January. Theoretically, the *Bibers* would simply slip from their loosened chocks as the U-boats submerged beneath them within range of the target, each *Biber* carrying two torpedoes. Once the attack was completed, the *Bibers* were to return to a rendezvous point off Sjet Navalock, contacting the 'parent' boats via short-range transmitter, then scuttle while

A Type VIIC U-boat returning to Trondheim harbour after a patrol. The medium-size Type VIIC was the backbone of the U-boat service during World War II, but was largely obsolete by the war's end despite numerous upgrades. (Naval History and Heritage Command)

the pilot was retrieved. If the rendezvous failed for whatever reason, the *Biber* pilots were to make for Persfjord and from there attempt to reach Sweden overland.

The three U-boats departed Harstad on 5 January with their cargo, running surfaced in the winter darkness. However, the perpetual vibrations caused by the diesels took their toll on the small *Bibers*, which in combination with heavy Arctic seas broke petrol lines aboard two *Bibers* and caused leaks on all of them once they were tested by submersion. Not a single midget remained seaworthy and they were subsequently abandoned and scuttled. Somewhat ironically, the intelligence report on which *Caesar* had been predicated was incorrect, *Arkhangelsk* having sailed to the White Sea days before.

The final U-boat lost within the Arctic was U711 on 4 May 1945, destroyed by bombs from Fleet Air Arm Avenger/Wildcat teams. British escort carriers HMS *Searcher*, *Trumpeter* and *Queen* were engaged on Operation *Judgement*, directed against the harbour at Kilbotn, where depot ship *Black Watch* and Norwegian steamer *Senja*, commandeered by the Kriegsmarine for use as an ammunition transport, were also sunk.

Oberleutnant zur See Hans-Günther Lange's U711 had been moored alongside *Black Watch* as the attack began. Frantically put under way by a skeleton crew that had been aboard, it was sunk mid-harbour. Lange and all 11 of his men escaped before U711 went down, while 40 others resting aboard the *Black Watch* were killed. Ironically, Dönitz had already ordered the end to operations earlier that morning:

> *'All U-boats cease fire at once. Stop all hostile action against Allied shipping. Dönitz'*

ANALYSIS

There is some merit to the idea that Germany's invasion of Norway was a strategic necessity, compelled by the need to foil a similar British intention. Securing the procurement and passage of valuable resources that were essential for the armaments industry was not optional, as without it, the Wehrmacht's requirements could never have been met.

Grossadmiral Raeder and even Hitler himself had desired a peaceful rapprochement with the Norwegian population, though in this they had greatly underestimated any nation's resentment towards being occupied by a foreign power. Undoubtedly, Reichskommissar Terboven's heavy-handed repression of the civilian population fuelled Norwegian anger and contributed to an exceptionally well-organized and effective resistance movement. It must also be noted that, though many written histories claim that Hitler desired the friendly cooperation of the local population, he did nothing to rein in Terboven's behaviour or that of the various SS agencies that went to work with gusto in Norway. Despite Boehm's best efforts as Commanding Admiral,

Norway to maintain a cordial relationship on the behalf of the navy with local Norwegians, it was never to be.

The invasion of Norway (covered in a separate volume) taxed the Kriegsmarine to the maximum; though successful, it left the surface forces heavily damaged and struggling to regain their previous strength, which had been woefully inadequate from the war's opening volleys. The idea of now possessing a strategically important location that provided a springboard for operations against the northern sea and entrance to the North Atlantic was soon nullified by Hitler's refusal to countenance a continuation of heavy surface ship sorties to the Atlantic after the loss of *Bismarck*. Despite providing an effective location for U-boats to refuel before breaking into the Atlantic, these were only forerunners of deployment in the French ports that provided proximity to the Atlantic battleground.

U-boat Arctic deployment was overall a failure. Though there were scattered successes – such as the near destruction of PQ17 – these were as much caused by tragically poor Allied decisions as good German ones. Conditions for all sailors of all nations within the Arctic could be appalling, and the terrifying prospect of being forced to abandon ship during the winter months spelled certain doom for any forced to do so. The Arctic convoys and their escorting forces battled bravely through these conditions, as did the Kriegsmarine and Luftwaffe crews who were attempting to stop them. However, in cold hard statistical analysis, the value of these Russian convoys was eventually more political than military. In terms of total wartime tonnage received by the Soviet Union, approximately 23 per cent arrived via the Arctic convoys, 27 per cent via the United States through the Persian Gulf, from mid-1942, and 50 per cent through the Pacific to Vladivostock, also from mid-1942.

However, this is not to denigrate the Arctic convoy route. In 1941, it was the only practicable method of assisting the Soviet Union, and both symbolism and military value compelled the establishment of the 'PQ' convoys, empty ships comprising 'QP' convoys headed back to Britain. In purely statistical terms, the Germans completely failed to impede the flow of supplies, sinking just over 6 per cent of the merchant ships that trailed from Britain to the Soviet Union.

Z33 under attack in Førde Fjord by Coastal Command, 9 February 1945. Four crewmen were killed. (Author Collection)

Sixteen Royal Navy warships were lost and several Soviet military vessels in and around the convoy route. In return, the Kriegsmarine lost one battleship, three destroyers and 30 U-boats in direct action against the convoys, along with many more in and around the Norwegian area. Equipment arriving in Murmansk during 1941 and early 1942 undoubtedly contributed to the defeat of *Silberfuchs*.

Maintaining German security of the Norwegian coastline both for the protection of essential German convoys and prevention of Allied raids ashore proved a herculean task that the Kriegsmarine was never able to fulfil. Though the coast became heavily fortified and bristled with both navy and army coastal artillery and flak artillery installations, the number of available security vessels and convoy escorts always lagged behind requirements. By late 1942, the Kriegsmarine was fighting on so many fronts in so many different geographical locations that it would never successfully meet the requirements for any one of them. The lack of resources – both personnel and equipment – that would bedevil the Wehrmacht in every theatre of action affected the Kriegsmarine presence in Norway hugely. Likewise, Luftwaffe requirements to provide effective reconnaissance, protection and anti-shipping missions would never be met. The Third Reich began the war understrength and largely unprepared. By 1942, the German war machine was exhausted and, though it may appear that it was still in a state of high tide, with the industrial power of the United States about to be unleashed and the vastness of the Soviet Union consuming men and materiel, it was purely a matter of time before Germany was defeated.

In Norway, the necessity to hold what Hitler came to believe was Germany's 'zone of destiny' and maintain the flow of resources to the Reich would use vast numbers of troops and equipment. Much of this spent most of the war idle and awaiting instructions. This is also true of many significant warships, particularly the *Tirpitz*. Hamstrung by the combination of lack of fuel and prohibitive orders that forbade risk, this mighty ship lay dormant. Though true that its potential danger at sea presented a threat to the Allies, its reality was symbolic of waste and missed opportunity. Morale and training standards suffered aboard such ships, arguably leading to such desperation on behalf of Dönitz to prove the large ships' worth that an unprepared *Scharnhorst* was lost in the disastrous battle of the North Cape, the war's final big-gun engagement between the Kriegsmarine and Royal Navy. *Tirpitz* fared even worse, ultimately destroyed by air power which had long eclipsed the 'big-gun navies', something that had been vividly proven during naval actions in the Far East.

FURTHER READING

Barnett, Correlli, *Engage the Enemy More Closely*, Hodder & Stoughton, London (1992).

Bauer, Arthur O., *HF/DF An Allied Weapon against German U-Boats 1939–-1945*, Diemen (2004)

Blair, Clay, *Hitler's U-Boat War, Volumes 1 & 2*, Weidenfeld & Nicolson, London (1999)

Boehm, Hermann, *Norwegen zwischen England und Deutschland*, Klosterhaus Verlag, Lippoldsberg (1956)

Brustat-Naval, Fritz & Suhren, Teddy, *Nasses Eichenlaub*, Koehlers Verlag, Herford (1983)

Churchill, Winston, *The Second World War* (6 Volumes), Cassell & Co., London (1954)

Dönitz, Karl, *Ten Years and Twenty Days*, Weidenfeld & Nicolson, London (1958)

Hessler, Günter, *The U-boat War in the Atlantic, 1939–1945*, HMSO, London (1989)

Hutson, Harry C., *Arctic Interlude: Independent to North Russia*, Merriam Press, Bennington (1998)

Kemp, Paul, *Convoy: Drama in Arctic Waters*, Arms and Armour Press, London (1993)

Lohmann, W. & Hildebrand, H.H., *Die Deutsche Kriegsmarine 1939–1945* (3 Volumes), Podzun Verlag, Bad Nauheim (1956)

Neitzel, Söhnke, *Die deutschen Ubootbunker und Bunkerwerften*, Bernard & Graefe Verlag, Koblenz (1991)

Paterson, Lawrence, *Hitler's Forgotten Flotillas. Kriegsmarine Security Forces*, Seaforth Publishing, London (2017)

Paterson, Lawrence, *Schnellboote. A Complete Operational History*, Seaforth Publishing, London (2015)

Paterson, Lawrence, *Steel and Ice. The U-boat Battle in the Arctic and the Black Sea, 1941–45*, The History Press, Cheltenham (2022)

Polmar, Norman, *Submarines of the Russian and Soviet Navies, 1718–1990*, Naval Institute Press, Annapolis, MD (1991)

Raeder, Erich, *Grand Admiral*, De Capo (2001); first published USNI 1960 as *My Life*

Rohwer, Jürgen, *Axis Submarine Successes of World War Two*, Greenhill Books, London (1999)

Rössler, Eberhard, *The U-Boat*, Cassell & Co., London (2001)

Whitley, M.J., *Destroyer*, Arms and Armour Press, Londons (1983)

Wynn, Kenneth, *U-boat Operations of the Second World War* (Volumes 1 & 2), Chatham Publishing, London (1998)

INDEX